Young Writers
2004 POETRY COMPETITION

ONCE UPON A RHYME

IMAGINATION FOR A NEW GENERATION

East Sussex
Edited by Heather Killingray

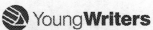 Young**Writers**

First published in Great Britain in 2004 by:
Young Writers
Remus House
Coltsfoot Drive
Peterborough
PE2 9JX
Telephone: 01733 890066
Website: www.youngwriters.co.uk

SB ISBN 1 84460 481 0

Foreword

Young Writers was established in 1991 and has been passionately devoted to the promotion of reading and writing in children and young adults ever since. The quest continues today. Young Writers remains as committed to engendering the fostering of burgeoning poetic and literary talent as ever.

This year's Young Writers competition has proven as vibrant and dynamic as ever and we are delighted to present a showcase of the best poetry from across the UK. Each poem has been carefully selected from a wealth of *Once Upon A Rhyme* entries before ultimately being published in this, our twelfth primary school poetry series.

Once again, we have been supremely impressed by the overall high quality of the entries we have received. The imagination, energy and creativity which has gone into each young writer's entry made choosing the best poems a challenging and often difficult but ultimately hugely rewarding task - the general high standard of the work submitted amply vindicating this opportunity to bring their poetry to a larger appreciative audience.

We sincerely hope you are pleased with our final selection and that you will enjoy *Once Upon A Rhyme East Sussex* for many years to come.

Contents

Bobbie Linton (8)   37
Niall Yeandle (9)   37
Jonty Sweetman (9)   38
Yousef Obied (9)   38
Brandon Fossey (9)   38
Jemma Fowler (8)   39
Kloe Ball (8)   39
Chelsie Mold (7)   40
Esmee Mercer (7)   40
Mariah McLean (8)   41
Lucy Summerfield (9)   41
Jemma Payne (8)   42
Kieran King (7)   42
Navdeep Kaur (8)   43
Al-Amin Miah (9)   43
James Fulker (8)   43
Courtney Torch (9)   44
Jazmin Greenfield (8)   44
Zachery Fossey (7)   44
Christopher Brown (8)   45
Waleed Obeid (7)   45
Gregory Lake (9)   46
Amy Williams (7)   46
Melissa Bowles (8)   46
Katie Hoey (9)   47
Thomas Gates (7)   47
Aldo A Michel-Villalobos (9)   47
Jordan Doyle (10)   48
Liam Ayto (9)   48
Alex Price (10)   48
Rachel Ward (9)   49
Sam Bean (10)   49
John Tibbs (9)   49

Highfield Junior School
Hollie Durrant (10)   50
Elleesha Phillips (11)   50
Christopher Clarke (11)   51
Louisa Sheeran (10)   51
Chloe Deadman (11)   52
Jordan Walder (11)   52

Little Common School

Tom Godfrey (11)	70
Chloe Denvir (10)	71
Emma Gooch (8)	71
Lewis Parker (11)	71
Nicholas Dupker (10)	72
Hollie Stinson (11)	72
Ellie Payne (11)	73
Christie Vaughan (10)	73
Zoe Bretton (10)	74
James Copper (10)	74
Jay Beckton (11)	75
Anastasia Payne (8)	75
Adam Foord (10)	76
Paris Whytome (11)	76
Zoë Woodcock (11)	76
Nathan Goldsmith (11)	77
Aaron Isted (11)	77
Daniel Rains (7)	78
Adam Rouncivell (10)	78
Maryann Hardingham (11)	79
Kate Alexander (10)	79
Jenny Whelan (7)	80
Thomas Harris (11)	80
Josh Glavin (11)	81
Imogine Thompson (10)	81
Lucy Tidey (10)	82
Megan Barton (10)	82
William Greenwood (11)	83
Nadine Long (10)	83
James Pfaff (11)	83
Eleanor Thorne (10)	84
Thomas Browne (8)	84
Giorgia Ribaudo (10)	85
Daniel Hope (8)	85
Rachel Frost (10)	86
Sarah Park (10)	86
Naomi Jarvis (10)	87
Tanya Hillman (10)	87
Charlie Horsman (10)	88
Carl Addy (11)	88
Taylor Mcfaile (9)	88
Brogan Moore (10)	89

James Roadknight (10)	90
Alexander Field (7)	90
Eden Parker-Demir (10)	90
Samantha Antolik (8)	91
Maddie Wilson (7)	91
Jenny Smith (11)	92
Robert Brighton (8)	92
Fiona Leggat (9)	93
Rebecca Pfaff (7)	93
Andrew Slinn (8)	94
Oscar Hammond (8)	94
Jodie Henningway (7)	95
Sophie James (9)	96
Amelia Harrison (9)	97
Katy Croft (8)	97
Olivia Davies (9)	97
Patrick Hills (8)	98

Middle Street Primary School

Molly Skelton-Greenwood (9)	98
Robyn Gall (10)	99
Sienna Gladwin (10)	99
Agnes Vaughan (10)	100
Jasmine Walker (10)	100
Heloise Payne (10)	100
Lauren Wheeler (10)	101
Ruby Lewis (10)	101
Mitchell Mulvay (10)	101
Jools Turner (10)	102
Daisy Barrell Shearer (9)	102
Rosa Steele (9)	102
Poppy Gandy (10)	103
Declan Hall (10)	103
Myles Keep-Stothard (10)	104
Ivy Klein (10)	104

Ninfield CE Primary School

Tazmin Barton (10)	104
Ben Jones (11)	105
Matthew Broadbent (9)	105
Sarah Campbell (10)	106

James Godden (10)   106
Hannah Caney (11)   107
Tabitha Hilton-Berry (10)   107
Sophie Connor (9)   107
Alice Smith (10)   108
Harriet Sinfoil (10)   108
Abbie Ballard (10)   109
Ryan Allen (11)   109
Leanne Newnham (11)   110
Anna Saxby Foster (9)   110
Alexander Mitchell (10)   110
Harry Saunders (10)   111
Adam Franks (11)   111

Patcham House Special School
Charlie Bennett (10)   111
Nathan Lovegrove (10)   112
Jack Wright (10)   112
Dave Upton (9)   112
Michael Patrick (8)   112
Kelly Gunn (10)   113
Sam Humphrey (11)   113

St Aubyns School, Brighton
Aston Peters (8)   113
Hugh Jeffery (11)   114
Aimee Barron (10)   114
Jessica Poulter (8)   115
Timmy Calliafas (8)   115

St Bede's Prep School, Eastbourne
Riya Nambiar (7)   116
Jamie Whelan (8)   116
Georgia Mae Ellis (8)   116
Jordan Thomas (7)   117
Gheorghe Richards (9)   117
Abigail Quinn (7)   117
Henry Miller (8)   118
Oliver Tingley (9)   118
Eleanor James (10)   119
Nick Salway (9)   119

St Mary's C Primary School, Brighton

Crystal Rodrigues (10)	135
Phoebe Thorpe (10)	135
Rhiannon Haestier (10)	136
Eleanor Dowds (8)	136

St Mary's RC Primary School, Crowborough

Henry Groenen (8)	137
Dominique Ollivier (9)	137
Peter Spyrka (8)	137
Bradley Goldsmith (9)	138
Joe Hicks (9)	138
Rebecca Hawkins (8)	138
Connor Plane (8)	139
Victoria Huxley (9)	139
Tom Nicoll (9)	140
Wren Lane (9)	140
Holly Barrett (9)	140
Karolina Chalk (9)	141
Joseph Reidy (9)	141
Henry Garrett (8)	141
Harry Dobson (9)	142

St Peter And St Paul Primary School, Bexhill-on-Sea

Ethan Martyn (7)	142
Arran Blows (8)	142
Oliver Woodward (8)	143
Amy Webb (7)	143
Rachelle Diedericks (7)	144
Jem Lewis (8)	144
Georgina Marston (8)	145
Daniel McKenna (8)	145
Ryan Johnson (8)	146
Matthew Fryer (8)	146
Daniel Gardner (7)	147
Paige Edwards (8)	147
Chloe Willis (7)	148
Connor Coshall (7)	148
Thomas Elphick (7)	149
Nathan Lopez (7)	150
Natasha Coda (8)	150

Willingdon Primary School

Rebecca Eaton (11)	167
Samara Lynn (9)	167
Kyra Dinnage (9)	168
Ellie Robinson (11)	168
Charlotte Yates (9)	169
William Leeding (9)	169
Rebecca Triggs (10)	170
Charlotte Golding (9)	170
Emma Le Teace (9)	171
Emily Ritchie (10)	171

The Poems

I Wish

I wish I knew if there were life on Mars,
I wish I could have my own way.

I wish I could have chocolate bars,
In my lunch every day.

I wish, I wish, I wish,
I wish, I wish, I wish.

I wish my family was rich,
I wish we had lots of money.

I wish I could go out on my pony,
Whenever it was sunny.

I wish, I wish, I wish,
I wish, I wish, I wish.

I wish I was a popstar,
With sexy, cool clothes.

I'd be so cool, I'd even pierce
My ears and nose.

I wish!

Jessie Whitehead (8)
Blacklands School

Fairies

Fairies fly high up in the sky,
Twisting and twirling as they go by.

Sparkles and glitter fall from up high,
The magic begins when they start to fly.

A flutter of wings and waves of wands,
They glide down low beside the garden ponds.

I wish, I wish, I wish tonight,
To be that fairy that shines so bright.

Shauna Johnson (8)
Blacklands School

My Cat

He's fat, orange, fluffy and old,
The cat poem is being told,
He sits around in the sun,
I bet he could eat a chocolate bun,
He's friendly, cuddly, kind and sweet,
He's as fat as an orange you could eat.
He's been run over once or twice,
I bet he could eat 100 mice.
At his birthday he would jive,
Even though he's still alive.
He tries to climb up the door,
And hangs on with his paws.
He tries to peep through the window,
But we won't let him in though,
In the glass he peeps through,
When we look we know who,
Two big eyes peeping out
A big miaow he lets out
All he wants in his tummy
Is tuna, fish, yummy, yummy!

Alice Rowe (7)
Blacklands School

Rainbow Poem

Red is like love in the air,
Yellow is the sounds of spring,
Orange is the taste of summer,
Blue is like rippling lake,
Green sounds like the seaweed smashing a rock,
Indigo smells of flower growing.

Courtney Neale (9)
Blacklands School

My Dog Nelly (Sometimes)

My dog is called Nelly,
She is very smelly,
She sits by the fire,
And sometimes watches telly,
When you say 'Paw'
She sometimes barks at the door,
When you say 'Sit'
She sometimes doesn't do it.

My dog is called Nelly,
She is very smelly,
When she eats lots of food,
She sometimes is very sick,
She goes to work with my dad,
And sometimes comes home black,
When we take her to the park,
She sometimes goes berserk!

My dog is called Nelly,
She is very smelly,
Her bed is in the kitchen,
She sometimes tries to sneak upstairs,
When we take her to the beach,
She sometimes swims and swims,
When you call her name
She sometimes runs away.

Nelly is mine,
But I love her all the time!

Joe Thomas   (8)
Blacklands School

First Child On The Moon

'Hello there
First child on the moon
What do you feel on the moon?'
'I feel the rocks on the moon,
All squishy like marshmallows.'

'Yes but first child on the moon,
What is it you can taste up so high?'
'I can taste the mud on the moon,
It tastes like Dairy Milk chocolate
So creamy and light.'

'OK OK child on the moon but
What can you smell way up on the moon?'
'I can smell fresh mud and fresh rocks way up there.'

'Alright, alright, tell us more -
What can you see up there little child?'
'I can see little brown hills like little mud castles and
Black holes like big long dark caves.'

'Now tell us some more, oh please tell
More what can you hear?
Is it noisy up there?'
'I can hear the wind whistling away
Like a train on the run,
Fading away and away.'

Ryan Harman (9)
Blacklands School

Weather

I like the sun,
I like the rain,
I like it when it's cloudy,
I like it when it's snowy,
I like the weather,
All of this is part of
The weather.

Aleishia Hurst-Gates (8)
Blacklands School

Who Am I?

Here comes the tallest lady
She walks with her head up high,
Her legs are walking sticks,
Her spots are big and wide,
Her tail is like a feather duster,
Her smile is as big as it can be,
And now she comes and bends right down
And eats right off me.

They eat bananas every day
Swinging off the trees,
Their tails are long and furry,
Sweeping away the bees.

Their smiles are big and cheeky,
Jumping off the vines,
Nicking my bananas,
Which were really mine.

He flies around all night,
Hooting all the way,
With big brown wings and pointed ears
He sleeps away the day.

With stretched out wings
He swoops through the air,
And catches little animals
And takes them to his lair.

I'm wondering if you have guessed
What the animal's are,
A giraffe, monkey and owl,
Have you guessed them?
Ha! Ha! Ha!

Lauren Gooch (9)
Blacklands School

My Dolphin

My dolphin is a bottlenose,
Over sea places is where he goes.

He is called Sundance because of his orange spot,
A simple grey and white dolphin he is not.

His mum Splash is now dead,
She used to love swimming in and out of the water bed.

Ever since Sundance's birth,
He has lived in the Moray Firth.

That's in Scotland, a long way away,
Where all the dolphins jump and play.

If I ever get the chance to go and visit him,
He would probably be shy and only show his fin.

Lisa Normoyle (10)
Blacklands School

Wish, Wish, Wish

I wish I had lots of money
I wish I had Dad with me all the time
I wish I could fly to the moon
I wish I had lots of sweets.

I wish I could fly to Chocolate Land
I wish there was no school
I wish to write in pen at school
I wish I could do something rather than think.

I wish I could stand on the moon,
I wish I could do whatever I want,
I wish I had another sister.

I wish, I wish, I wish.

Adam Hull (8)
Blacklands School

I Wish . . .

I wish I could fly like a bird,
Swooping in and out of trees,
Like a kite in the wind,
I wish I could fly like an aeroplane,
Skimming in and out of the clouds,
Like a pebble on water.
I wish I could fly like a glider,
So peacefully, without any noise
Like a fish swimming in the water.
I wish I could fly like a swan,
Beautiful and white,
Like roses falling from the sky,
Fluttering down,
Down,
Down,
I wish . . .

Alastair Hunnisett (9)
Blacklands School

Snow

I like Hastings in the snow,
It makes my fingers want to glow,
I love my garden all glistening white,
The snow makes everything sparkly bright,
But some grown-ups do not like the snow,
Because they think their cars won't go!
But all the children in my class,
Love the snow and want it to last,
(Forever).
So grown-ups, don't worry about your car,
Go for a walk in the snow,
It isn't far!

Abigail Osborne (7)
Blacklands School

In The Morning

Quickly quickly,
Line up straight
Sorry sir I'm very late,
Mum woke me up with a cup of tea,
But my bed was so comfy.
I laid and laid till Mum said,
'Wake up, wake up sleepy head.'
I brushed my teeth and washed my face,
I felt like I was in a race,
I went downstairs to eat my toast,
I like jam on it the most.
We jumped in the car and zoomed off the drive
It shouldn't take us long to arrive,
Here we are at the school gate,
Sorry Mr Ridings, I'm a bit late.

Sophie Homewood (8)
Blacklands School

Magical Potion

Magical potion:
One frog that leaps,
One mouse that peeps,
One black cat's claws,
One white rat's paws,
One elephant's tail,
The slime of a snail,
A small child's dream,
A midnight scream,
Mix it all up and
Put in a cup,
It should be lucky,
But urgh! It's yucky!

Paige Warden (7)
Blacklands School

From A Space Rocket

We looked back at the world,
Rolling through space
Like a giant moon with a calm
Cool, silver face.

All its cities and countries
Had faded from sight,
All its mountains and oceans
Were turned into pure light.

Slowly, its noise and troubles
All seemed to cease
And the whole world was beautiful and silent
And endless peace.

Ryan Mockridge (8)
Blacklands School

Coco The Cat

Coco the cat is very, very fat,
He's extremely lazy and drives me crazy,
He sits on my bed and squashes my head,
He takes up all the space,
Puts his tail in my face,
He's a bit of a pest but I love him the best.

Flora Davenport (9)
Blacklands School

Butterflies

Butterflies, butterflies everywhere,
Beautiful butterflies floating in the air,
Red ones, yellow ones, some with brown spots,
Some are tied in terrible knots,
Summer time is coming and I can't wait to see
What a wonderful joy it will be for me.

Thai Turner (8)
Blacklands School

Please Mrs Kerby

'Please Mrs Kerby,
This girl Louise View,
Keeps drawing on my work, miss,
What shall I do?'

'Go and sit on another table dear,
Throw it away and start again,
Go and sit on the carpet my flower,
Do what you think is best.'

Lucy Anne Kerby (8)
Blacklands School

Mouse

I had a mouse
I called her Willow
She used to play on my pillow
I'd clean her out with my mum
Me and Willow had lots of fun,
She's run around my bed
And poo on my floor,
I had to be careful and
Always close my door.

Emma-Lee Thomas (8)
Blacklands School

Snakes And Others

Snakes slide,
Snakes sliver
And snakes hiss!

Lions whiz,
Lions sneak
And lions roar!

Daniel Pascoe (7)
Blacklands School

I Want To Be . . . An Artist

I want to be an artist
I don't know what to do
I could paint a picture
Or make a sculpture out of you.
My teacher says use oil paints
My friends don't really care
I think I will use oil paints
Because I'm in despair.
I want to do a landscape of our school,
Should I do the field or the swimming pool?
I want to be an artist
But I don't know what to do.
I think I should not worry,
But I'm really, really sorry
Greens and blues, it's hard to choose
What colours I should use.
My teacher's going on at me
Showing me perspective things
I've got to make my mind up soon
Before the bell rings.
I'm in a dream world of my own
I can't do my work
I'm very bored
I want to talk
I have a headache
I'm going home
I will not fret
I do not care
I don't want to be an artist
I want to be a vet.

Rhiannon Nother Carter (9)
Blacklands School

Six Little Mice

Six little mice lived in a wood,
Six little mice, so pretty and good,
Their tails were long, and their eyes were bright,
And they loved to flit in the pale moonlight.
But Mummy Mouse shook her head, and said,
'My dears you're safer by far in bed,'
But the very next night,
When the moon shone bright,
They forgot their promises and
Stayed out that night,
They knew that owl was on her
Nightly proud way,
She pounced on one, she pounced on two,
With a loud toowit and a hoarse toowoo.
She carried them off, that owl, so brown
And their poor little tails came dangling down,
Away they scampered, the frightened four,
But two little mice came home no more . . .
And the owl's brown babies up in the tree
Had mouse for dinner,
And mouse for tea!

Jordan Wright (9)
Blacklands School

A Party Song

Merry have we met
And merry have been,
Merry let us part,
And merry meet again.

With a merry sing-song,
Happy, gay and free,
With a merry ding-dong,
Again we'll happy be.

Demi Brockington (8)
Blacklands School

I Wish, I Wish

I wish my sister didn't boss me about,
I wish I had my own bedroom,
I wish my sister didn't shout,
I wish I had a monkey that would
Swing from the trees.

I wish I could escape to Neverland,
I wish I had a different name,
I wish my big sister wouldn't tease me,
I wish I could fly like a bird in the sky.

I wish I had a dog of my own and a kitten too,
I wish I could walk to town on my own,
I wish I had a bowl of sweets ready to be eaten,
I wish I was popular and have lots of friends.

I wish I had no brothers and sisters,
I wish I had a baby sister or brother,
I wish all the world was full of girls,
I wish I had a nearer grandma.

Godith Hawkins (9)
Blacklands School

Christmas Is . . .

Christmas is a time for sharing,
Christmas is a time for caring,
Christmas is a time for praying,
Christmas is a time for playing,
Christmas is a lump of snow,
Christmas is a cheerful glow,
Christmas is a star above a stable,
Christmas is a pie on the table,
Christmas is a lot of red,
Christmas is children tucked up in bed.

Dominic Everett-Arnarsson (8)
Blacklands School

Space Stars

S pace is dark, it's hard to leave a mark,
P lanets spinning round and round,
A liens I can see coming towards me,
C omets flying past my spaceship,
E xciting, my very first space adventure.

S tars on the move,
T winkling in the distance,
A stronauts floating going up and down,
R ockets zooming past,
S olar system moving fast.

Joanna Standen (9)
Blacklands School

Christmas

C hristmas is a time when you're given toys,
H aving toys for girls and boys,
R ings of tinsel over there,
I magining that you were here.
S anta's sack is full of toys,
T oys for all good girls and boys,
M aking toys for girls and boys,
A t last Santa's sack is full of toys,
S o let's all go to bed!

Clara Pascoe (8)
Blacklands School

I Wish I

I wish I could fly like Peter Pan,
I wish I could go to the moon,
I wish I could be the ocean,
I wish I was royal,
I wish I didn't wear glasses,
I wish I was a helpful, beautiful girl,
I wish I didn't have freckles,
I wish I was very good,
I wish I was like God,
I wish I could walk on water,
I wish I had my grandad back,
I wish I could play with him.

Shelbi Annison (9)
Blacklands School

Untitled

I have a friend Karen Jane,
She lives in a house down the lane,
We do everything we can together,
And go for walks collecting heather,
We share all our troubles and joys,
Often going shopping for clothes and toys,
We often laugh at silly things,
Also talk about our dreams,
Often cry together when we're glum
My best friend is my mum.

Sian Curtis (9)
Blacklands School

I Wish

I wish I could fly up to the clouds,
I wish my mum brought ice cream
I wish my sis wasn't loud
I wish my mum wouldn't clean
So I could mean.

I wish my toys were nice,
I wish school was fun,
I wish my sis chucked out the mice,
I wish I could hum.

I wish I could eat lots of sweets,
I wish I was cool,
I wish for lots and lots of treats,
I wish I had a swimming pool.

Sarah Steel (9)
Blacklands School

My Best Friend

My best friend is called Samantha,
Her favourite animal is a panther,
She doesn't like veg,
But likes her bed,
She likes parties
Especially if they're arty,
She wears lots of make-up,
But doesn't like wake-ups,
She doesn't like boys,
But loves toys,
She likes food
But doesn't like shoes.

Sophie Normoyle (8)
Blacklands School

My Ted

Ted is mine
Ted is cuddly
Ted sits on my bed all day
I love my ted!

Ted is brill
Ted is lovely
Ted keeps me safe all night long
I love my ted!

Ted is soft
Ted is squashy
Ted's been sewn up lots of times
I love my ted!

Ted is torn
Ted is battered
Ted has been pegged on the line!
I love my ted!

Ted is blue
Ted is white
Ted's fur has all worn away
I love my ted!

Ted is old
Ted is floppy
Ted was Mum's when she was young
I love my ted!

Ted is a friend
Ted is special
Ted cheers me up if I'm sad
I love my ted!

I love my ted best of all
And best of all . . . ted loves me!

Claire Barham (8)
Blacklands School

Untitled

Robins sitting on a post smelling the smell,
Robins hear the music as well,
What a special time of year
Because it's Christmas time.
Children singing Christmas songs,
Mummy's baking yummy pies,
What a special time of year,
Because it's Christmas time.
People eating special dinners,
Special dinners because it's
Christmas time.
What a special time of
Year because it's Christmas time.
People putting their Christmas tree up
With baubles and a
Little fairy too.
What a special time of year
Because it's Christmas time.
Children love it when they open presents
It's the nice thing to do
What a special time of year
Because it's Christmas time,
People play in the soft thick snow
Building snowmen or angels,
Or making cakes for me and you.
Then we jump in the car and
Drive home, we step out of the car,
I love to sleep in my bed,
I fell asleep and softly said goodnight.

Sophie Wong (8)
Blacklands School

Sorry

Hello sir, I'm very sorry
My car got stuck behind a lorry,
A car sped out of a turning.
Now my tyres are really burning.

Then my dog spotted a bone,
All day long he didn't groan.

Now I am explaining why I'm late,
All my friends won't want me as a mate.

Emily Grace Bridger (8)
Blacklands School

The Sun

Sun, sun glorious sun,
How I wish to be you.
Your hair, your eyes,
Your lips tingle like the
Shimmering moon.
I need the sparkling
Cheeks as soft as the
Rain falling into a bucket of
Ice cream.

Hermione Hawkins (9)
Blacklands School

My Brother

When Jordan eats his chocolate,
He smears it on his face,
He gets it everywhere you see,
He smears it all over the place,
I can't see through the windows,
Or through the doors, it's everywhere,
Oh my goodness, it's on his underwear!

Lauren Hearn
Broad Oak Community Primary School

My Flower Poem

I love yellow flowers on my window sill,
Especially when I'm lying in bed feeling rather ill!
When I have to take a medicine pill,
I like to look at the yellow flowers on my window sill.

I love blue flowers on my bedside table,
Which hide all the disgusting electricity cables,
I like to read my books at night,
Especially my favourite fables!
I love blue flowers on my bedside table.

I love red flowers sitting upon my shelf,
Right next to my collection of tiny elves!
My mum likes to keep us all in good health,
Especially by putting red flowers on my shelf!

Katy Atkinson (10)
Broad Oak Community Primary School

Midnight Feast

I have it with my friends and me
When I have a midnight feast
I always get the chocolate all around at least,
I always get it everywhere, everywhere you see,
Now oh my goodness I can't even be.

I should not of done this, I should not of done
But at least the house is now melted from the sun,
Now my mum is angry now my mum is cross,
But now I have a new room
I have it with my friends and me
When I have a midnight feast.

Elizabeth Woods (9)
Broad Oak Community Primary School

Christmas Eve!

C ards and presents
H olly on top of tasty puddings
R acing round in the snow
I ndoors cosy and warm
S nowmen standing proud and tall
T rees getting decorated with bright colours
M ince pies cooking in the kitchen
A ngel sitting on the huge tall tree
S tockings full of lovely presents.

E ventually Santa gets here
V ase filled with smelly flowers
E veryone says goodbye to Santa.

Amy Swan (9)
Broad Oak Community Primary School

Summer Days

S un, hot and yellow,
U nder a shady tree,
M unching happily on your picnic,
M eeting friends to play with
E nd of the day is near,
R unning about in the flowers, playing hide-and-seek.

D ays swaying side to side
A nd you are running wildly, but now it's time to rest,
Y ou are going to have your dinner,
S leeping soundly and happily waiting for a new day.

Sophie Calderbank (9)
Broad Oak Community Primary School

The Man That Gallops

The shadow that gallops through the night
The sharp wind chases till night.

When the first full moon is set
All night long in the dark and wet.

Why does he gallop and gallop?

The trees bend over, he gallops aloud,
The wind makes a sound like a swirling cloud.

When the sun is set, he gallops with the night,
Until he comes back just after light.

You ask yourself 'But who is the man that
Gallops?'

Charlotte Davies (9)
Broad Oak Community Primary School

Horses

Big ones, small ones, fat ones, thin ones,
And round stumpy ones,
Grass and carrots all stuck in the gums!

Grey, white, black and dun,
So many colours, the more the fun,
Oats and barley, an apple treat,
Horses and ponies say yuck to meat!

Gymkhana, races and more,
Horse riding is never a bore,
In all weather, sun and rain,
Riding along clinging onto the mane!

Fran Stallman (10)
Broad Oak Community Primary School

Different Children

Outside on a winter's day the trees tremble,
Frightened by the wind,
Inside children dancing happily around a burning fire,
Outside poor and lonely children peer in through the window,
Inside children's laughter bellows around the room,
Outside the children's faces fall to the ground,
Never remembering their own birthdays.
Inside their clothes blend with the colourful floating balloons,
Outside the rags droop to their feet,
Blending with the gloomy dull sky,
Inside excited faces notice glum downhearted
Children longing to come in.
Outside they no longer feel isolated,
Inside kind-hearted children feel generous,
Inviting them in.

Oliver Rowlatt (9)
Broad Oak Community Primary School

Under The Stairs

Under the stairs, in the dark,
Sat an old mouse called Mark,
He had a big grin,
And he had a big chin.

He had an orange tail,
And ate all the mail.
He liked playing ball,
And he ran into a wall.

He sits in a box,
And he gets attacked by a fox,
Dickory dickory dock
He got stuck up the clock.

Jack Long (9)
Broad Oak Community Primary School

My Birthday Party

I woke up on my birthday pleased as a punch,
When I saw my cake, I was overjoyed and I ate
It in one munch,
Then my friends arrived, I felt very jolly
And I danced around with my friend named Polly,
Soon it was time to go, I felt very glum,
Don't be sad they can come again said my mum.

Kath Coleman (10)
Broad Oak Community Primary School

All Alone

All alone, in a room full of nothing, but air,
Nobody there, nobody listening, nobody even cares.
You shout out, 'Where are you?' Nobody replies,
They said they would return, but that was just lies,
They said they would call, but they never did,
All alone, the only one in the room is you,
Alone, waiting.

Alex Goodsell (10)
Broad Oak Community Primary School

Mummy

My mum's hair is short, silky and orange,
Her eyes are twinkling and sparkling
And her skin is soft and speckled.
She has got an empty china basket
With three flowers on the front
Which is on a black stand
On top of the fireplace
And it is really special to her.

Katie Reeve (7)
Charters Ancaster College

Dragon In The Kitchen

A dragon
Switched on . . .
He hums very low
Lying in wait
For you to open the door
So that he can
Breathe fire!

A wiry tail
And a mouth wide open
To burn his innocent victims
To ash.
His clawed feet stand rigid
And lie in wait.

Then he sleeps,
Switched off,
Cold, silent, stiff
And motionless
Waiting.

Daisy Reece (9)
Charters Ancaster College

Snowman

Slushy snowman,
Slippery ground,
Cold feet!
Oh, look what we've found?
Looking over the garden fence
Icicles hanging from next door's bench.
Oh look, to my surprise!
A snowman in front of my own eyes.
Do you know what fun it is
When winter comes again?

Tessa Patterson (8)
Charters Ancaster College

In My Head

In my head there is a pencil
Scratching at my brain,
A horse cantering
And red lights
Flashing.

In my head are purple curtains
Opening and shutting,
Butterflies flapping their enchanted wings
And bull frogs jumping
Up and down.

In my head is dreamy music
Being played and making me cry
And memories waiting
For the right moment
To surface from the depth.

Eden Richards (11)
Charters Ancaster College

Dangers In The Forest

The hippo,
Stomping slowly,
Huge as a mountain,
Moves like an earthquake,
While the frog
Is small, poisonous and spotty
And kills quickly
If you touch it!

Benjamin Hammond (10)
Charters Ancaster College

Kitten

Big and small
And sometimes tall,
He sits and lies
Warm and cosy
Smooth and silky
Sleepy and sleek
Washing his paws,
Purring . . .

But . . .
Watch out!
Sometimes
He is snooty and independent
And turns into
A snapping tiger
Biting
Hissing
And
Fizzing!

So next time you see a cute, sweet kitten . . .
Beware!

Katie Hatter (8)
Charters Ancaster College

The Snake

The snake is a volcano,
Slithering like lava
As it spits over its ghastly fangs.
Sometimes it lies dormant
Coiled, sleeping in its home
Later grabbing and killing
With its poisonous venom
Erupting
Then calming down
To make a smooth and glossy surface.

Alice Newnham (9)
Charters Ancaster College

Evil Spell

A cockerel's beak and a pair of smelly feet
Throw in the pot before it gets hot.
The bubbles fly and pop
But the mouth of the snake says 'Stop!'

Tail of tiger and robin's wing
Start our potion with scorpion's sting.
Voice of owl and a snow hound's howl
Put together to bake.

Then add the ear of man
And the nose of a hairy ape.
Tooth of rabbit and lizard's tongue
To destroy all the fun.

Next we change the sky from blue
So it matches the colour of green goo
Now the ground must leap in the air
To turn the clouds the colour brown.

Finally life must start to turn
So we put in a fairy burn
The bone we use to stir the potion
Puts in a revolting lotion.

At last the Earth is under my control . . .
Ha! Ha! Ha! Everyone has a cold!

Daniel Ogilvie (10)
Charters Ancaster College

Recipe For A Dragon

Take a bowl of lava with ten lizards alive in a cage
Add the lizards into the lave, then some sharp teeth,
Scales, eyeballs and a box of matches.
Stir in a cupful of blood and a teaspoon of clear water,
Decorate with a pork chop, green knives and an alligator's tail
Bake for one hundred years and you will have a dragon.
Take care!

Stephen Kennedy Redmile Gordon (8)
Charters Ancaster College

The Alligator

Pointing and slicing through the water
Chopping and cutting through the current
Thrashing in the cold liquid
Is the king of rivers and lakes.
The crocodile's brother
And close friend of the caiman.
He strikes with that powerful jaw,
Whips with that awesome tail,
A fearsome blow,
A deadly shock.
He tears at a lifeless carcass
Chewing the flesh hungrily.
The vultures come scavenging.
The extreme emperor rules the waters
With a fierce hypnotic stare.

Matthew Pope (10)
Charters Ancaster College

The Snow Tiger

The snow tiger walks softly,
Jumps and floats gently down
Eating up the melted crystals.
Soaring fast
He slithers quickly
And pounces.

The snow tiger walks softly,
Plods and twirls playfully around
Following his black paw prints.
Roaring loudly
He circles, trying to catch his tail,
And pounces.

Isobel Kellett (8)
Charters Ancaster College

The Train

The long snake
Lives in a dark hole.
Soon it will wake up
And be on its way,
Eating all sorts of people
That get caught every day.

It slides and slithers along the tracks
Gliding on straight lines,
Wiggling on the bends.
Grey smoke and steam
Rising into the air
Hissing and whistling,
Waving and spitting,
Twisting and turning,
Then squeaking wheels . . .
As it comes to a stop.

Dale Knight (9)
Charters Ancaster College

Granny

My granny has curly, short hair,
Rough, creamy skin
Wrinkly, blue eyes
And she smells like rosy perfume.
We play long, hard games
Of Scattergories and Newmarket
She is a really good player.
My granny likes telling me very important secrets.
My best memory was when she came out of hospital,
She says in a posh voice,
'This house is as clean as crystal'
My granny is cool
She is like a tall, white crocus.

Patrick Pope (8)
Charters Ancaster College

The Plane

Swooping, diving
The big bird flies
Stretching sliver wings
Spread out so far.

Swooping, diving
Faster and faster
Catching tasty prey
To eat.

Swooping, diving,
Searching the undergrowth
Looking for movements
People to catch.

Swooping, diving,
Through the turbulent air
On its way to lands
Far away.

Swooping, diving
Its rumbling roar
Echoing above,
Soaring through the cloudless sky.

Rosie Reeve (10)
Charters Ancaster College

Recipe For Happiness

Weigh out some fluttering, red butterfly wings,
Sieve in the touch of a kitten's silky fur and
The fluffy coat of a dog
Chop in some blue sea looking like a wavy mat.
Add in the creamy taste of chocolate
Slowly fold in the soft whisper of the wind
And the sound of the doorbell
Mix all together and bake until well cooked.

Jackson Poole (8)
Charters Ancaster College

That's You And Me

As friends we:
Play
Sleep
Run
And share each others thoughts over
A bit of lunch.

As friends we:
Jump
Skip
Read
And play our favourite games together in
The playground.

As friends we:
Run
Play
Eat we play football together at lunchtime
And play our favourite music together too.
One girl, one boy,
Together forever we stand forever with
Each other, by each others side
Forever, one lock, one key, forever
We stand by each others side.

Alix Green (8)
Coldean Primary School

Friendship

It's a snowy day,
It's a game of snowballs,
It's a warm pair of mittens,
Shared by two friends.

Christopher Middleton (8)
Coldean Primary School

Friendship

It's a special moment,
It's a long life story,
It's someone who you can rely on
And a piece of glory.

It's a valuable friend,
It's someone who's there,
It's someone to stay with
And always care.

It's a roller coaster,
It's someone who's kind
It's a funny feeling
And hard to find.

Marcos Millet-Martison (8)
Coldean Primary School

Friendship

It's someone who's kind,
It's someone who's there,
It's someone with you,
It's someone to share a pear.

It's someone who cares,
It's a long life story,
It's a big favour,
It's a piece of glory.

It's a person you'll play with
It's someone you trust
It's someone that's nice
It's a big gust of wind.

Harry Robinson (8)
Coldean Primary School

That's You And Me

As friends we:
Run,
Giggle,
Jump
Then we play around with football
And lots of games.

As friends we:
Skip,
Sleep,
Walk,
Then we sleep over friends,
And we play games like rugby.

As friends we:
Talk,
Play,
Whisper,
Then we talk and whisper
And we watch TV.

Scott Cooper (7)
Coldean Primary School

Friendship

It's watching a movie,
It's a bowl of ice cream
It's a scary story,
That makes you scream.

It's play in the park,
It's a seat in the shade,
Swing on the swings,
Help when I'm afraid.

Jamie Schooley (8)
Coldean Primary School

That's You And Me

As friends we:
giggle,
play,
run

We run to get our friends,
then we play a game of football.

As friends we:
swim,
walk,
play

We joke around,
as we go to the cinema.

As friends we:
skate,
jog,
joke

Then we skate and have fun.

Samuel Brooker (8)
Coldean Primary School

Wall Of Water

Waves crashing like dinosaurs walking
Rolling and spitting foam up the beach
Heavy waves, boats dangerous,
Devastating wall of sea water,
Waves crashing on rocks,
Blue strong sea water,
Clatter, shatter whoosh.

Cameron Newman (7)
Coldean Primary School

That's You And Me

As friends we:
smile,
share,
giggle
then we play outside all day
and do the things we love.

As friends we:
skip,
run,
play
then we play rounders in the playground,
and play games that we love.

As friends we:
swim,
sleep,
and read
then we play all day long,
and share our treats.

One boy
one girl
one friendship to enjoy
one key
one lock
that's you and me.

Daniel Bushby (8)
Coldean Primary School

That's You And Me

As friends we
play,
giggle,
read,
then we go together
to the park to play.

Charlotte King (8)
Coldean Primary School

Friendship

Friends are special
Like my best friend.

Tell her a secret -
She doesn't tell.
Play games with her at lunchtime -
Getting on well.

Politeness, understandingness,
Never falling out.
Screaming round the playground,
Laughing when we shout.

Getting on together,
Sharing our ideas.
Bestest friends forever,
Never any tears!

Bobbie Linton (8)
Coldean Primary School

Friendship

It's a kind person to play with
It's a happy sight
It's not a bully
but not a stranger to be with at night

It's someone to eat with
It's someone to trust
It could be an animal
to nibble off the bread crust

It's a person who helps
It's someone who's a biker
It's not a man in a costume
but his nickname is Striker.

Niall Yeandle (9)
Coldean Primary School

Monkey King

He eats the jungle fleas
He swings on loose branches and falls
He messes with gorillas, gets kicked to rivers
And falls down the waterfalls
Now he's so wet
I think I'll have a bet
That he catches the flu
Ahh Choo.

Jonty Sweetman (9)
Coldean Primary School

The Sun

As bright as
fire. The biggest thing
in the world. A dangerous
poison with fire, as still as
a rock. The strongest
thing ever.

Yousef Obied (9)
Coldean Primary School

That's You And Me

As friends we:
play
giggle
cuddle
then we play football
and we sleep over.

Brandon Fossey (9)
Coldean Primary School

That's You And Me

As friends we:
share
walk
play
then we dance into the night,
listening to our favourite music.

As friends we:
jump
run
joke
then push each other on the swing,
and pick flowers.

As friends we:
write
draw
colour
then dream and dream until we wake up.

Jemma Fowler (8)
Coldean Primary School

Fireworks

Frizzing like sherbet
Always go wee, pop, bang
They are colourful
They are beautiful
They go into a shape
They are always cheerful
Diving like a rat
Squeaking like a mouse
Whizzing like racing cars
Always goes bang like a party balloon.

Kloe Ball (8)
Coldean Primary School

That's You And Me

As friends we:
run
giggle
smile
then play together every day, morning and night,
and sing together.

As friends we:
play
read
eat
then watch the moonshine,
and go bowling.

As friends we:
walk
share
sleep
then share our thoughts,
and to love.

Chelsie Mold (7)
Coldean Primary School

Left Out

I feel like a bomb
I'm going to explode
I can't feel my feet
and I'm starting to
feel the beat of my heart
pounding when people
say nasty things
and I feel cross.

Esmee Mercer (7)
Coldean Primary School

That's You And Me

As friends we:
run
play
skip
then we skip across the playground
doing what we like.

As friends we:
read
eat
jump
then we eat in school
bored and stiff.

As friends we:
giggle
talk
hop
then we hop down the
playground stairs.

Mariah McLean (8)
Coldean Primary School

Snake

Slimy, large, smooth snake
he slithers through the grass
over a log and into
a pond and river, he stretches
his body and shines his scales
slimy snake.

Lucy Summerfield (9)
Coldean Primary School

That's You And Me

As friends we:
giggle
run
laugh
then slide down the bank,
laughing very loudly.

As friends we:
jump
swim
play
then we go swimming very loudly,
acting like maniacs.

As friends we:
sleep
read
share
then we sleepover each other's house,
and share each other's sweets.

Jemma Payne (8)
Coldean Primary School

The Storm River

The river runs free down between
the banks when we see
the honey-bees collecting pollen
for their tea.

Then the storm comes crashing
and the river begins to rise
the water starts splashing and bashing
breaking against the rocks.

Kieran King (7)
Coldean Primary School

Water

Wet and damp
Soaking sprinkle
Drizzling and blue
Cold and drenched
Smashing spray chuckles
Splashing, freezing
Cold and slippery
Drip, drop
Pouring and flooding.

Navdeep Kaur (8)
Coldean Primary School

The River

The river is freezing cold,
It gushes through the middle,
The cunning river never stops for a rest,
It's an endless stream.
The crew never gets apart,
Don't tumble in,
Or it might drag you away.

Al-Amin Miah (9)
Coldean Primary School

River James

Strong as the sea,
Splashes down strong as the gigantic
Sea, waves, moves. a slight movement,
Skipping over rocks swiftly,
Moves gently with the fishes,
A singer, as he dances along.

James Fulker (8)
Coldean Primary School

Me And Myself

Me and myself are playmates.
We will never leave each other's side.
We are friends forever.
Me and myself are neighbourly.
Wherever I go my friend goes.
Whatever move I make my friend does it too.
Me and myself.

Courtney Torch (9)
Coldean Primary School

Snow

Cold and icy,
as white as a polar bear.
Melting in your hand,
clean as a sheet.
Crunching under your feet.
Snowflakes floating from the sky,
covering the land.

Jazmin Greenfield (8)
Coldean Primary School

Left Out

I want to punch the air
Because I am angry
I'm left out of the game
I put my head on my folded arms
I don't want you to see me cry.

Zachery Fossey (7)
Coldean Primary School

Snow

Snow
makes you
shiver and
freezes the
liver, and
then the
animals
hide well away from the
tide, it
shoots from the sky as
fast as a
fly, it covers
the town and
people frown.
It covers the trees
and makes you
sneeze, it scratches
your nose but
people are
sad when
it goes.

Christopher Brown (8)
Coldean Primary School

The Old Farm

The ducklings snuffle
the big cow ruffles
at the old farm.
The baby sheep is running
around the old farm.
The big pig has a wig
the funny sheep is acting
like Bo-Peep.

Waleed Obeid (7)
Coldean Primary School

Untitled

Snowy mountain-tops glisten in the sun
Zig-zagging down, having lots of fun
Riding back in the cable car
Oh, my word, how far
Toboggan really fast
I hope this fun can last.

Snowmen I love to make
It's a piece of cake
When there's lots of snow
We'll have a go
And make him six feet tall
As long as he doesn't fall.

Gregory Lake (9)
Coldean Primary School

At School

My day starts at school
My work just piles and piles
I go outside and meet
A friend, then we have
A game of ball.

Amy Williams (7)
Coldean Primary School

Left Out

It feels like a volcano of tears
exploding in my eyes. Like I'm someone
else. I feel upset when people pick on
me. Like I didn't want to be born.

Melissa Bowles (8)
Coldean Primary School

My Family

My mum is dumb,
My dad is mad,
My sister Kat is a rat,
My brother Shane is a pain,
So when I need help with homework,
English, maths, humanities too,
I really don't know what to do,
But some days I have to
say, 'I really, really love you.'

Katie Hoey (9)
Coldean Primary School

Friendship

It's another you
It's a nice smile
It's a shadow of you

It's a voice in your head
It's a helping hand
It's someone to trust
It's someone to play with
It's someone to count on.

Thomas Gates (7)
Coldean Primary School

Puppies

Puppies are cute when they play with you,
puppies are fast when they chase a cat,
puppies are funny when they chase a bunny,
but the best thing about puppies, they'll grow up
and still play like a puppy.

Aldo A Michel-Villalobos (9)
Coldean Primary School

My Cat

My cat is very fat
My cat always sits on my lap
My cat will eat anything
My cat will play with string
My cat lives in my house
My cat chases the mouse
My cat is very small
My cat always falls off my wall
My cat is cute
But my cat plays the flute
On Monday she looks all fluffy
But on Sunday she looks all scruffy.

Jordan Doyle (10)
Coldean Primary School

Creatures

Some creatures are small
Some creatures rule,
Some creatures are thin
Some creatures are dim,
Some creatures are rare
Some creatures grow up in a pair,
Creatures are all shapes and sizes
And many have different disguises.

Liam Ayto (9)
Coldean Primary School

Poem

Some people dream of being rich
and driving a fancy car, but for
me there is no contest - you're my
favourite dream by far.

Alex Price (10)
Coldean Primary School

England Football Club

When we kick the ball,
We sometimes fall.
Michael Owen scores,
And sometimes roars.
David James dives,
And a goal arrives.
From the England team we say 'Bye',
And the crowd say 'Why?'

Rachel Ward (9)
Coldean Primary School

A Day In The Life Of A Monkey

Monkeys live and swing in trees,
Dodging and eating ripe, green leaves.
Monkeys are hairy, with long arms and legs,
To help them swing through the trees,
To get to their beds.

Sam Bean (10)
Coldean Primary School

The Football Match

Football, football is so cool,
Because you get to kick a ball,
Up and down the pitch you go,
The crowds swaying to and fro,
All at once a goal is scored,
Oh, how the people roared.

John Tibbs (9)
Coldean Primary School

Being A Child

Being a child is not so bad
But even sometimes I become very sad
In life there is so much to do
Going to New York with you

I often wonder why it is
That my friend is called Liz
Travelling is easy in these modern days
Travelling the world in 80 days
Being a child is not so bad

I've been around the world in 80 days
The weather was great
I never want to go on holiday again
Because I am happy now
I wish I was a child again
Growing up to be clever
Being a child is not so bad.

Hollie Durrant (10)
Highfield Junior School

The Tooth Fairy

I have a mushroom at the bottom of my garden,
Where I think the fairies live.

I sat there and sat there,
Making sure nothing got out of my sight,
But no fairies appeared that night.

I went to bed thinking of the tooth fairy,
Wondering if Mummy and Daddy were right.

But then I thought they had to be right,
As someone takes my tooth away at night!

Elleesha Phillips (11)
Highfield Junior School

The Trupetmuizes

The trupetmuizes are red and black
They come in all shapes and sizes,
Some are green and some are blue
And some have a lot of surprises.

But trupetmuizes have no care at all
They don't care about a thing,
But when it comes to food that's different
Their ears begin to sing.

The trupetmuizes live in the woods
They're very, very small,
Sometimes they're so crazy
They'll drive you up the wall.

They walk around all day
Eating bugs and spiders,
But now you'll find them
Right down beside us.

Christopher Clarke (11)
Highfield Junior School

Valentine's Day

Valentine's Day is all about love,
A couple who share what they have with each other.
Valentine's Day is all about love,
A couple who share their dreams with each other.

Valentine's Day is all about love,
But not everybody has someone
To love, so only some people celebrate
Valentine's Day.
Valentine's, Valentine's, is my love,
Kiss me now and pick me up and take me away.
Have a meal or two, let me come home
In your arms and your comfort!

Louisa Sheeran (10)
Highfield Junior School

Spots

I hate growing up
Because there's something you get
A small kinda lump
That you get on your head
It's all kinda pussey
You stay in your bed
Your mum starts to nag
So you cover your head

One morning Mum gets up
And is delighted to see
You scrubbing your face
But there's a problem, you see
Where there was one spot
There's suddenly three
These horrid spots
Seem to be growing on . . . *me!*

Chloe Deadman (11)
Highfield Junior School

I Wish

I wish I had a dolphin
That was black, blue and grey,
And was long, smooth and shiny
I'd swim with it all day.

I wish I had a dolphin
To play with in the waves,
We'd swim amongst his fishy friends
And find some secret caves.

I wish I had a dolphin
To swim with in the sea,
I'd cuddle it and care for it
My best friend it would be.

Jordan Walder (11)
Highfield Junior School

School

School is so boring
6 hours of work
So mad in the morning
But at home time, a smirk.

School is so boring
Maths and literacy
But I love art and music
Science and PE.

School is so boring
Most boring in the world
Out of all the competitions
I've never won what they held.

School is so boring
But at home time it's fun
As I fight with my brother
Until the set of the sun.

Kieran Farnes (10)
Highfield Junior School

Feelings

Everybody has something that makes them feel warm inside.
It may be a person, animal or toy,
That makes them feel warm inside, cosy, loved, and takes away their
loneliness
And makes them feel warm inside.

What makes you feel warm inside, cosy, loved?
Something that takes away your loneliness,
Is it a person, animal or toy?

Lauren Hunt (11)
Highfield Junior School

School

School is cool, we
Learn a lot, if
We mess about, we get
Sent to time out, if
We're good, a great
Career and a life full
Of fun and cheer.

Daniel Black (10)
Highfield Junior School

Travelling

I love travelling
A horse and cart
Carries me away
On my tour
The racing traffic passing by

I love travelling
A train carries me away
To the beach
The warm breeze passing by.

Charlotte Dean (10)
Highfield Junior School

The Desert!

The desert is the sun glowing every minute of the day,
The desert is the heat baking everything away,
The desert is the camel's life.

Cassie-Louise Holdsworth (10)
Highfield Junior School

Toys

My teddies always keep
A close eye on me while I sleep,
They have a *big* secret
That they never will tell . . .
That they come alive at night
In case they give me a fright

My dolls in my dolls' house never even move
At night they have a party
And always dance the groove

Even my baby dolls
Start crawling and
Pretend to be moles.

Nicole Robertson (10)
Highfield Junior School

Cats' Eyes

Cats' eyes are bright,
they sparkle in the moonlight.
They glow in the dark,
you can find them in the park.
Cats' eyes are sharp and clear,
you can see them far and near.

Cats' eyes are blue and green,
they love to be seen.
Cats are great,
they are the animal you shouldn't hate.
Cats live in houses and in the street,
I think cats are *neat.*

Ashley Phillips (10)
Highfield Junior School

What's In The Teacher's Drawer?

What's in the teacher's drawer?
Maybe a Double Decker?
Or twenty glittery hairspray cans?
Or one hundred and ten confiscated shoot-out cards?
What's in the teacher's drawer?
What's in the teacher's drawer?
Maybe a chocolate wrapper from a Crunchie?
Or there might be a mouldy apple core?
What's in the teacher's drawer?
Maybe some smelly socks and trainers?
What's in the teacher's drawer?
Do you know?

Emily Lindsay (10)
Little Common School

Purple And Pink

I love pink and purple,
I love purple and pink,
All the boys in my class think those colours stink.

I've got lots of pens with purple ink,
I've got lots of pens with pink ink.

I have pink in my bedroom and purple on my bed,
When my mum asked what colours I want

I said, 'Pink and purple or maybe
Blue instead.'

Megan Sumner (9)
Little Common School

My Puppy Pepsi

Pepsi's cute, Pepsi's new
Pepsi's black, Pepsi's true
Pepsi's playful, Pepsi's a licker

My puppy Pepsi is a *winner!*

She wags her tail when she is happy
She plays tug-of-war until she's scruffy
She then settles down on her bed
And rests her little black head

My puppy Pepsi, I really love her.

Charlotte Streeter (10)
Little Common School

The Best Brothers And Sisters

My big brother is very nice
he lifts us up really near the sky
he is only 14 years old.
My big sister is the best
she is 9 going on 16
but my little sister
is the most loving sister.
My other big brother
is horrible.

Beth Chapman (8)
Little Common School

My Cat Is Fat

My favourite cat is called Strika,
He has ginger fur.
When I stroke him gently,
He begins to purr.

Anthony Laidler Huggett (7)
Little Common School

When I Got The Monster Toe Stuck In My Ear

One day I was in my room,
When I heard a *bing, bang, boom!*
I crept to the door,
Guess what I saw.

It was big, it was brown,
It was in a gown.
It had razor-sharp claws,
And massive jaws.

It jumped on my head,
As though I was dead.
It jumped in my ear,
And knocked my gear!

I went to the doctor and he said, *'Hi!'*
He said, 'The best thing for it is a rub of pie.'
So I went home and bought a pie,
I crept through the door and hoped I'd die.

I rubbed the pie on my face,
At a slow pace.
The toe came out,
And I yelled a big . . . 'yelp.'

Conal Groves (10)
Little Common School

My Balloon Ride

As I went up, I could hear the air
funny though, I was just on the fair
down below, people on rides
flying around like flies
as I grew taller
down below, people got smaller.

Katie Horscroft (9)
Little Common School

Safari Holiday

Early morning excited, peering through our long-distance binoculars,
Bumping up and down, our binoculars stuck in our foreheads.
There, in the distance, we think it is a rock or, we drive closer,
I can't believe my eyes, then we see its white princely, leathered body.
Bumping along a long, dusty road,
Aloe Veras every which way we look.
Hello, here comes an ostrich, with its long spindly legs,
Then we see it's just had too much to eat.
Roaring lions sleep and laze around,
I thought they would do something, but it just looks like they can't.
Scared as the trumpeting elephants have us in the corner of their eyes,
Just thinking about if the elephants are going to crush us.
Lightning, there goes a wildebeest, storming right across the road,
Playing with his friends.
Sad, say goodbye,
Goodbye to all the wonderful animals that I have seen today.

Nicola Chapman (10)
Little Common School

The Sea

The sea is bright, so go and have some fun
Turtles are swimming by
Dolphins are leaping as if they could fly
Whales looking for food

Get your bucket and spade
And have some fun
Enjoy the beach
And all that is good.

Nicole Maynard (8)
Little Common School

Months

January
Snow is falling to the ground
Snowflakes spinning round and round.

February
Nearly spring, but not just yet
Almost time to see the vet.

March
Beginning of spring, but still cold
The farmers have new lambs, I've been told.

April
Showers, rain, rain, rain
Let the sun come out again.

May
Dancing around maypoles
Rabbits are popping out of holes.

June
Daddy's birthday, hot and sunny
All the bees get lots of honey.

July
Off we go, out of school,
Time to go in the swimming pool.

August
Hot and sunny, all my friends
Are rather funny.

September
Here we go, back to school
All the boys are rather cool.

October
Hallowe'en, ghosts and fear
Trick or treat is almost near.

November
Leaves are falling from the trees
Time of year for a sneeze.

December
Dark time of year, but full of light
Stars are twinkling in the night!

Sophie Doick (8)
Little Common School

In The Rainforest

Little brown monkeys
Swinging in the trees,
Grabbing mates' backs
And scratching at fleas.

Flying through the branches,
Shooting down the vines,
Hairy brown monkeys
Dancing in lines.

Munching on passion fruit,
Spitting out the pips,
Acrobatic monkeys
Doing lots of flips.

Sun sinks down now,
Up comes the moon,
Little brown monkeys
Sleep until noon.

Thomas Knapp (11)
Little Common School

The Strange House

Once upon a time
There was a house,
It stood on a hill,
All very still.

It looked very bleak,
The roof had a leak,
The house was very weak
With a scary creak!

The front door was green,
The windows looked mean,
The rooms were dark,
Was it what it seemed?

Inside that house,
As quiet as a mouse,
Lived an old man,
Whose name was Sam.

Rebecca Pitman (11)
Little Common School

I Love School

I love school
I never break the rules
my mummy drops me off at 20 to 9
and kisses me goodbye.

First we take the register
to check everyone's there
and we get ready for the lessons
by sitting on our chairs.

The day consists of learning
which can be lots of fun
literacy, numeracy and spellings
and then the day is done.

Jade Vause (8)
Little Common School

Rabbits

Rabbits hop
Rabbits jump
Rabbits go thump, thump, thump
In and out, round and round
Thumping to the tiny beat.

Rabbits hop
Rabbits jump
Rabbits eat not much junk
They love to make new friends all day
On a happy, sunny day.

Katie Wolford (7)
Little Common School

Polar Bear

Growl as loud as a lion's roar,
Fur as white as a cotton wool bud,
Nose as black as a coal on the fire,
Ears as soft as a kitten's tail.

Tummy full of wet, flapping fish,
Eyes as glittery as a marble in the sun,
Leather pads underneath his paws,
He is a polar bear.

Poppy Lelliott (8)
Little Common School

Leprechauns

Leprechauns are such strange creatures,
They're very small and green,
With pointy ears and big top hats,
They're the strangest thing's I've seen.

Kit Beale-Wharton (10)
Little Common School

My Little Pony

I had a little pony, he ran very fast,
I groomed him every day.
When we went in races, he was never last.

I call him Mr Dumbledore,
I feed him lots of hay,
He has a very shiny coat,
He loves to run and play.

I like to ride my pony,
He is my bestest friend,
He never bucks or bolts with me,
I'll keep him to the end.

Michelle Agoston (11)
Little Common School

Snow

Fluffy snowflakes swishing through the air.
People playing without a care.

Snow is fun
Snow lets you play with everyone
Snow is crisp
Snow is cold
Snow is great.

Nathan Jay (8)
Little Common School

Pizza

I can eat pizza anywhere.
In the cupboard.
On the stairs.
I can eat it anywhere!

Sam Aharchi (10)
Little Common School

Monsters

Mum, I'm scared
Of going upstairs,
The boogie man might be waiting there.

Mum, do I have to go?
Please say no.
Gramp the cramp might be there,
Do I have to go?

But Mum, I'm really scared
Of going upstairs
To find a great black spider
Drinking all the cider.

Do you really have cider?
No, it's the spider.

Kestrel McMullen (10)
Little Common School

My Hamster

I sleep in a comfy house,
But some people think I'm a mouse.
I'm gnawing at my cage
With a little bit of rage.

I run miles and miles in my wheel at night,
When it's dark and nobody is in sight.
I'm running in my ball,
Feeling really cool!

I'm on my top level,
Feeling like a devil.

Scott Sherwood (8)
Little Common School

My Poem

The sunshine was there shining bright,
Shedding far its glistening light,
Always high in the sky,
Never-ending love for us,
Always there without a fuss.

It's there all night shining bright,
Wishing for day and then for night,
The moon is there with help from the sun,
No one knows when its days began,
The day will come when it will stop,
That day might rain, drop, drop, drop.

The weather changes every day,
Sometimes cold in the month of May,
The sun is hiding, hiding away,
Not sure when it's warm again.
Then again it might snow,
But I'll get colds and have to go.
The weather changes every day,
But you never know, it might snow today.

Nicole Benson-Feathers (10)
Little Common School

My Bedroom

My bedroom's purple, like the colour of sunset.
It's got a bunk bed full of sweets and junk.
There's bookshelves full of videos to watch,
But the most important thing of all
Is a cupboard with my clothes.

Ceri Hawkins (7)
Little Common School

The Google Bird

Did you know that there is a bird called a google,
That comes from outer space?
It rather looks like a poodle,
And it's here to wipe out the human race.

It's red, yellow and blue,
With a pointed black beak.
With a head like a kangaroo,
It skips from feet to feet.

For breakfast it eats meat,
And for lunch it eats shoes.
It sees that as a lovely treat,
And now it's after *you!*

If I was you today,
I'd stay at home in bed,
For as the sky turns grey,
It won't wait until you're dead.

Do not be alarmed,
As it only feeds in June.
Until then you'll be unharmed,
Until you hear the google bird's tune.

It'll strike at the stroke of midnight,
Just like an angry bear.
You'll be in for a terrible fright,
And also a terrible scare.

With a flap of its wing
It will be off in a flash,
If you say the magic words,
Bish!
Bosh!
Bash!

Luke Webster (11)
Little Common School

Christmas

C old, shivery snow that comes at the frozen winter
H olly that hangs on doors and windows
R ising snow that comes now and then
I vy which is known well at Christmas
S ilver tinsel that tingles all around the house
T owns all lighted with twinkling lights and decorations
M erry Christmas screams Santa on his floating sleigh
A ngels that fly down on Christmas Eve
S trips of gleaming lights all around the world.

Tonia Chapman (9)
Little Common School

Flowers

F ruitful smelling through the air,
L ittle flowers growing in the hot air,
O ver time they are colourful and bright
W hen they grow, they're big and bright,
E vening time then they close up,
   and in the morning they're back to normal,
R oses are bright and rosy-red,
S unflowers smile like Christmas morning.

Amy Horscroft (8)
Little Common School

Charlie

C harlie is my puppy,
H e likes to run around
A ll day he gets into mischief and
R aces across the ground, and he
L ikes to lie in the sun and
I like to lay with him, and his
E ars are all sloppy.

Jack Burridge (11)
Little Common School

Best Friends

B est friends, even if miles apart, stay in touch no matter what
E very day the bond becomes stronger in the alliance
S o what if challenges come our way and
T est our patience and flexibility?

F orever we may not be
R est assured we will find our way
I nto perfect harmony
E ach finding our own path
N either of us forgetting our
D earest friend and childhood
S o even after oh so many years, we're still the greatest of friends.

Douglas Gordon (11)
Little Common School

Football

F ootballers in the premiership have their
O wn shirt with their name and number
O n the back and they have a sponsor like
T -Mobile. When they get on the pitch, they kick off the
B all to start the game.
A ll the time they are kicking and passing to get their
L eading striker to score a goal. When he scores they
L eap on him and cheer and shout.

Jonathan Black (11)
Little Common School

All About My Cat Spit

My cat Spit used to spit,
His miaow is funny because
He just goes, 'mit'.
Watch out for my cat Spit,
Because he just might . . . *spit!*

Emma Cross (8)
Little Common School

Snow

I woke up this morning to find it was snowing,
All around was crystal and glowing.
We wrapped up ready to go out,
We stepped out of the door,
Slipping and sliding, down the hill,
On the pavement we felt we were gliding.
Got to school safe and sound,
Hope tonight we have some more
To cover the ground.

Josh Barham (11)
Little Common School

December

December is cold, dark and damp,
Like giving the world an ice-cold clamp.
Christmas comes on the 25th day,
Decorations, presents, that's the way.
When it snows children play
In the streets till the end of the day.
December is great as you hear,
It's a shame it only comes once a year.

Tom Vincent (11)
Little Common School

If I Were A Fish

If I were a fish
I would not wish
To be a fish
Because I would be a fish
And if I were a fish
I would probably be a fish
On a dish.

Tom Godfrey (11)
Little Common School

The Sun

The sun is busy, the sun is brilliant.
The sun works hard up in the sky.
He works together, to find
Different ways to shine.
His colour is bright,
His shape is round like a football.
Everyone can see him,
But why can't we hear
His crackling and the fire?

Chloe Denvir (10)
Little Common School

Fun In The Sun

Playing in the sun is fun.
Eating ice lollies
Dripping down my arm
Playing in the water,
Splishy, splashy,
Splish,
Splash,
Splosh!

Emma Gooch (8)
Little Common School

Black Arts

Bad magic lurks around,
It gives you bad luck wherever it's found.
Black arts are mean,
They can't be seen.
No one ever likes them.

Lewis Parker (11)
Little Common School

Poem About Computers

Computers can be useful,
But sometimes cause you stress.
I like the e-mail most of all,
Or playing games as well.

I become the characters,
Racing cars around the track.
I fight the baddies with a gun
Until they are all dead.

For homework there is publisher,
Or Microsoft Excel,
But you can make a Christmas card,
Or party invitations.

Nicholas Dupker (10)
Little Common School

Anyone, Yes Anyone, Can Write A Poem!

People have poems that are happy
And some are sad,
Some are about animals,
Anyone, yes anyone, can write a poem.

They are fun to write,
But sometimes you will get stuck for ideas.
Some are good at writing them, some are bad.
Anyone, yes anyone, can write a poem.

Other people get their inspiration from different places.
Some people write about their favourite thing.
I think poems are fun to write.
Anyone, yes anyone, can write a poem!

Hollie Stinson (11)
Little Common School

Night And Day

Sun's bright light is fading now
And starlight starts to peep.
The people on the Earth below
Will settle down to sleep.

So silver is the night so bright,
The moon is shining down,
The stars up there are winking at me,
So silver is the town.

How beautiful it is above,
Comets whizzing by,
Lighting up the air
And zooming through the sky.

A golden glow appears in the east,
And then the birds start singing.
The world is slowly awakening,
A new day is beginning.

Ellie Payne (11)
Little Common School

Winter Thoughts

Once upon a stormy sky
I looked up and saw an eye,
Looking at people rushing to and fro,
With busy lives they come and go.

Children's laughter fills the air,
No more worries, no more cares.
In their mothers' arms they cuddle,
Leaving the kittens in a muddle.

Time ticks by as we grow older,
Summer's gone and winter's colder.
In the playground we remember
Throwing snowballs in December.

Christie Vaughan (10)
Little Common School

Friday

Friday afternoon,
You never come too soon.
The class bell rings,
Everyone cheers and sings.

Charging past the teacher we go,
No one's ever slow!
My homework's due on Monday,
But I won't do it till Sunday!

Everyone's talking about their weekend ahead,
And how they can't wait to sleep in, in bed!
People planning to go out with their friends,
The chatter never ends!

Oh, Friday afternoon,
You never, ever come to soon!

Zoe Bretton (10)
Little Common School

The Snowman

I made myself a snowman,
As big as he could be.
I made myself a snowman
So he'd be a friend for me.

I made myself a snowman,
I thought I'd call him Fred.
I made myself a snowman,
And kept him warm in bed.

I made myself a snowman,
And a pillow for his head.
Last night, Fred ran away,
But first . . . he'd wet the bed.

James Copper (10)
Little Common School

Bunnies

Fluffy pink bunnies,
With love hearts for tummies,
Honeybees
With knobbly knees,
The pollen they pick
Will make you sneeze.
The rabbits were cute,
But started to recruit,
They gathered an army,
But all went barmy.
They tortured all the men
In groups of ten,
They started production
Of weapons of mass destruction.
They destroyed the Earth,
For all it was worth.
They murdered Mars
And blew up the stars.
When they were done,
They flew to the sun,
They reached in their pockets
And pulled out some rockets
And blew it to kingdom come.

Jay Beckton (11)
Little Common School

Dolphins

Splish, splash, splosh,
Go the dolphins
Under the cool, glistening,
Sparkling, crystal, dark sea.

Playing chase with each other
With their tails flipping,
In the water, gliding
In every direction.

Anastasia Payne (8)
Little Common School

Egypt

E gypt is a lovely place with tombs of pharaohs
   like King Tutankhamun and Queen Nefertiti.
G ods of *Egypt* come to life, Anubis and Amusi help me.
Y ou're the best, Tutankhamun, with your gold mask
   and your gold coffin.
P ower to you in the underworld, pass the trial of death
   and become free for the afterlife.
T utankhamun was the youngest pharaoh. He became
   king at 10 and died at 18, what a pity.

Adam Foord (10)
Little Common School

Dolphins

D ipping, diving, swimming, all the sports they do,
O rchestras have never caught the melody of their song,
L azing in the sun, waiting for the moon to shine,
P laying secretly under the coat of waves,
H appily jumping in and out of the sea,
 I 'd love to be a dolphin swimming through the sea,
N eat and tidy, curving their swift bodies around the rocks,
S lippery and silky is their skin.

Paris Whytome (11)
Little Common School

Animals

A is for the animals in the whole world
N is for the naughty kittens that chew at the furniture,
 I is for the iguanas that live in the hot sun,
M is for the menacing millipedes we have in the garden,
A is for the alligators with big, snapping jaws,
L is for the lion, king of the jungle,
S is for the snakes that slowly slither across the sands.

Zoë Woodcock (11)
Little Common School

How Do Planes Stay In The Sky?

Australia, Antarctica, China and UK,
They're just half of Mr Plane's whole day.
He can fly really high,
He touches the light blue sky,
But there's just one thing I don't understand,
How does he fly?
Does he fly with a string pulling him up,
Or is it just a secret way?
I don't understand.

His wings keep him gliding,
His engine keeps him moving
And his propellers keep in smoothing,
His face is long so he can go along
The light blue sky.
He can travel at five hundred miles an hour.
Gatwick, Heathrow, they're quite good airports in London,
Mr Plane goes there to meet new people.

Nathan Goldsmith (11)
Little Common School

Monkey Business

The only thing monkeys do all day
Is swing from the high treetops,
No work, just play.

Eating bananas all day long,
Breakfast, lunch, tea and dinner,
Singing their monkey song.

Every monkey in the gang
Loves to be tickled,
Especially the orang-utan.

Aaron Isted (11)
Little Common School

Friends And Family

Friends and family are always kind,
They are like a team which is combined.
They make me laugh,
They make me cry,
They make me usually sad when they say goodbye.

Friends and family are helpful to others,
Dads, mums, sisters and brothers.
They are always loving,
They are always caring,
And usually they don't mind sharing.

Friends and family are always there,
My mum's so cuddly, like a bear.
My sister is small, but she thinks she's tall,
I pick her up if she is to fall.

Friends and family mean lots to me,
They will be with me for eternity.
My family and friends will be there forever,
They will be there for me and each other.
I will try my best
To be a good son, friend and brother.

Daniel Rains (7)
Little Common School

Super Parents

If I had super parents,
They would be so cool,
They would have a swimming pool.

If they got paid a lot,
They wouldn't give a baby a cot.
They would give it something more,
Because they are not poor.

They can fly
And they will never die.

Adam Rouncivell (10)
Little Common School

Theatre Magic

All the cast are warming up,
All the orchestra are tuning up,
The theatre is all nice and clean
And the stage is set with a scene.
The show is ready to start.

Lots of people get excited,
Looking at the stage nicely lighted.
The audience sit on their seats,
Clutching their scrumptious treats.
Lights slowly go down, it's as dark as the midnight sky.

The audience love the show,
They don't want to go.
They have lots of fun,
But when the show is done,
They still keep on clapping.

Not really wanting to rise from their chairs,
Time to leave in groups or pairs.
Empty wrappers litter the floor,
The cast and orchestra leave from the stage door.
The theatre is dark, but the magic still remains.

Maryann Hardingham (11)
Little Common School

Friendship

Friendship is a roller coaster,
It always has its ups and downs.
Friendship is a tube of glue,
Sticking people together.
Friendship is like building a tower,
You never know how far it will go.
Friendship is when you have someone's name
Engraved in your heart.

Kate Alexander (10)
Little Common School

Diving Beneath The Waves

We're diving into the deep blue sea,
My mum, my dad and me!
We're floating around and we all wish
To find some interesting types of fish.

Swaying seaweed twirling around,
Fish swim past without a sound.
Angel fish are playing all around our feet,
And the sea horses are searching for something to eat.
A big red starfish snoozing on a rock,
Then a crab crawled out and gave us a shock!

We've swum around the deep blue sea,
My mum, my dad and me.
This day has been the very best,
And we all deserve a good long rest!

Jenny Whelan (7)
Little Common School

My Friend Charlie

My friend Charlie loves his hair,
He couldn't do anything if it was bare.
He slicks it down,
Like wet leaves to the ground.

He must have charismatic powers,
You can watch him on end for hours and hours!
He laughs a lot and tells a good joke,
Whilst captivating all the folk.

He is a trendy sort of guy,
So he doesn't wear a tie.
I gave him a beanie hat to wear,
But he threw it back because it messed up his hair!

Thomas Harris (11)
Little Common School

Grandma On The Motorway

My grandma and I were going to London one day,
But we had to go on the motorway.
So we got in the car,
And went to the bar,
Had a few drinks and set off.

We were on the motorway going very fast,
And I was afraid that I might need a cast,
Dodging every car and lorry,
Until we saw,
Oh no . . .
It was the old bill,
Waiting at the top of the hill.

'Can I see your driver's licence please?
Oh, and give me your keys.'
But my grandma didn't want to give them her keys,
So, she gave them her driver's licence as they said please,
But drove off with me and the keys.

We drove back home twice as fast,
And by that time I did need a cast.

PS This is not my grandma.

Josh Glavin (11)
Little Common School

White Tiger

She walks as gracefully as a bride
In a white dress, full of pride.
Her eyes are as blue as the deepest sea,
Her feline movement is clear for all to see.

She is graceful but powerful in one simple move,
We all know she has nothing to prove.
She flashes a warning with her smile,
Then she'll pounce, but still with style.

Imogine Thompson (10)
Little Common School

Tomato Soup

I hop to the shop,
I crawl to the mall,
I hate going shopping, it's no fun at all.
Tomato soup
Is on aisle two,
Just can't push my trolley through.
I moan when I get there,
It's just unfair,
Cheese or ham, I just don't care.
I moan about crisps,
I moan about jam,
I moan, moan, moan.
That's the way I am.

Lucy Tidey (10)
Little Common School

The Moon

The moon has a face
That grins at you in the dark,
Staring at you with his unblinking eyes,
Yawning and plodding slowly along,
Silently, making no sound.

The Moon frowns,
When only half his face shows,
Soundlessly thinking of thoughts.
The moon is distraught,
When none of his face shows.
Nobody thinks he is there.

Megan Barton (10)
Little Common School

Football

F licking the ball
O n to my knee,
O h no, offside.
T owards the shiny ball,
B reezing past defenders,
A n attacker strikes, he
L obs the goal,
L ovely finish.

William Greenwood (11)
Little Common School

Feeling

F eeling
E mbarrassed and
E dgy, they
L ove and
I nflame, they
N ever
G row old.

Nadine Long (10)
Little Common School

Cars

Fast cars speeding down your road,
Alloy wheels,
Metallic paint,
Double exhaust,
Twin turbo,
Massive spoiler,
Roof down,
Music blaring.
Boy racer!

James Pfaff (11)
Little Common School

Witch's Spell

Magic twirls, swirls and bubbles,
One day this spell will cause trouble.
Throw in a rattle of a snake,
Then a delicious, mouldy cake.
Eye of cat
And wing of bat!

Magic twirls, swirls and bubbles,
One day this spell will cause trouble.
Throw in a scale of armadillo,
Then a leaf of an ancient willow.
Bark of dog
And croak of frog!

Magic twirls, swirls and bubbles,
One day this spell will cause trouble.
Volcanic lava flows and flows,
Round and round the cauldron goes.
As black as night,
As foul as a septic cobra's bite,
Magic twirls, swirls and bubbles,
Today this spell will cause trouble!

Eleanor Thorne (10)
Little Common School

A New Season

The moon has gone down
and the sun is rising.
Snow has melted,
daffodils are blooming.
The birds chirp in the trees,
lambs are being born on the hill.
People are paddling in the sea,
and a spring breeze is in the air.

Thomas Browne (8)
Little Common School

Spook School

As I slowly and silently creep through the school,
I come across a dark classroom and slide in.

There are bats hanging from the dark, shadowed ceiling,
And the billowing curtains give away that they are ghosts.
The vampire in the mirror is staring around,
But nobody except me knows.

There are terrifying spooks in all of the cupboards,
The glowing pumpkins are placed on the walls,
But nobody else knows but me,
Nobody else at all.

There are monster books on all of the shelves,
And the paper's alive, I just know it,
But nobody else knows but me,
Nobody knows I'm scared.

There are savage pencils in all of the pots,
And the photos of kids are evil,
They are smiling a spiteful smirk at me, twisted and horrible,
It feels like there are hundreds of eyes, spooky as can be,
But nobody else knows at all,
Nobody else but me.

Giorgia Ribaudo (10)
Little Common School

Toys And Games

Don't know which to choose,
computer games, Bionicles or Yu-Gi-Oh!
They are all so good.
Some, you need other people to play,
Murder In The Dark, Operation and Connect 4.
Some you can play by yourself.
Most of all it is best to play with friends.

Daniel Hope (8)
Little Common School

The Birthday!

Grandma, I just want to say
A big, happy birthday.

I send you many birthday wishes,
Lots of love and tons of kisses.

Standing in your party dress
You may have to, no, you *do* impress.

I know you've reached that big 60,
So now's the time to really let go.

So shake your bottom,
Swing your hips,
Boogie to your fingertips.

You are great,
You're a smartie,
So come on Grandma, it's time to party!

Rachel Frost (10)
Little Common School

Our New Arrival

He whines and cries most of the night,
Sometimes he will put up a fight.
He loves to have lots of cuddles,
A few times he's made lots of puddles.

He eats and drinks lots, just like us,
Most of the time he has some fuss.
We clean him, feed him, all that sort,
He has been so very well taught.

He plays all day at any time,
I wouldn't sell him, not for a dime.
He is a very playful dog,
He won't touch a big, big log.

Sarah Park (10)
Little Common School

A Dancer's Life

The first day I went dancing,
I can remember well,
I was so keen and eager,
I tried so hard I fell!

But now that I am older,
I have to try and learn,
That when I go on to the stage,
I must attempt to turn.

And now that I'm eleven,
I have to exercise,
Just to make sure I have
A chance to win a prize.

As I hear the music start,
I execute a spin,
Then I leap across the stage,
I really hope I win.

And now, I am twenty-one,
I'm glad I earn my wage,
By doing what I love so,
Which is dancing on the stage!

Naomi Jarvis (10)
Little Common School

The Crocodile

Granny had a crocodile sleeping on her bed,
He went snap, snap, and chopped off Granny's head.

Granny has survived, although it seems untrue,
She lived to smile another day, and that I swear to you.

Granny had a crocodile sitting on her chair,
He went snap, snap, and ate her teddy bear.

Teddy is feeling better now, his head's been sewn back on,
He's even got a new name now, Granny's called him Ron.

Tanya Hillman (10)
Little Common School

Arsenal FC

A rsenal are the best, better than the
R est! They have great football skill,
S o they don't pay a bill.
E ven I think, oh, Arsenal rule don't they so!
N either black nor blue,
A rsenal rock, unlike you.
L osers like Liverpool have no chance to beat Arsenal.

F ootball is an exciting game, the best of them all.
C ome and join in the fun, the best sport you fool!

Charlie Horsman (10)
Little Common School

Volcano

V iciously the top of the mound explodes,
O ver-spilling and pouring down the sides, the
L ava flows, glowing red with heat.
C louds of smoke and steam fill the air,
A ll that can be heard is the ground rumbling inside.
N othing remains, it is all covered in molten rock,
O bliterating everything in its trail.

Carl Addy (11)
Little Common School

Pig

Sometimes I sit in the mud
With one eye open, snorting and grunting,
It must be time for another doze.
Waiting for the farmer
To bring me some food.
My mate Jess wants to play
But I'm not in the mood, only for food.
Jess nudges me with her wet snout.

Taylor Mcfaile (9)
Little Common School

An Unusual Family

My mum is spotty,
My dad is dotty,
My sister loves Orlando Bloom,
My brother stays locked in his room.

My auntie, she just loves stripes,
My uncle's favourite word is *cripes!*
My nana, she just pries and peeps,
My grandad, all he does is sleep.

My cousin just steals all my stuff,
My second cousin is just too rough.
She tips me upside down and shouts,
'That's what life is all about!'

My grandma two just loves rice pud,
I really, really wish I could,
Tip it upside down and run,
She'd shout, 'Tim, you ruined my bun!'

I'd shout back I didn't care,
About her silly, ruined hair.
My grandpa two just laughs and laughs,
While Grandma two just baths and baths.

My goldfish, he just likes seeing,
The world from inside his big blue,
And though some people say we do,
We don't all sleep in one big hall.
So you see, we're not such an unusual family after all.

Brogan Moore (10)
Little Common School

Music Is fun

M usic is a magical art,
U nveiling our hearts' desires,
S o close to silence or an ear-splitting noise,
I t is impossible to dislike music,
C lose to adored by some and enjoyed by others.

I deal for loving, or so it seems,
S pirit-shattering sounds and great fun.

F unny most music sounds, but some sound sad.
U ndo your mind with unexplainable feeling or dance to the beat,
N eedy will no longer be depressed with a golden sound like music.

James Roadknight (10)
Little Common School

Egyptians

They built pyramids great and fine.
They wrapped up mummies line after line,
They pulled the brain out through the nose,
Right by where the Nile flows.
They rode their camels across the sands
And carved hieroglyphics with their hands.
For their pharaohs they buried jewels and gold,
I'm not surprised why they're fairly old.

Alexander Field (7)
Little Common School

The Relic

It stands there old, chipped and wise,
Engraved with words and symbols,
All shapes and sizes.
The jagged shape creates a power,
A screaming hiss begins to lower,
The relic stands all shaped to glow.

Eden Parker-Demir (10)
Little Common School

At The Beach

I'm at the beach watching the waves,
I'm at the beach in the sand,
I'm at the beach making a sandcastle,
Oh no, a storm, I have to go home.
I think the lightning talks to the thunder
And the thunder replies.
Oh look, the sun's come out again,
I can go back to the beach with my friend.
We can look at the rockpools,
We can find some baby crabs,
We can go swimming in the sea.
I'm at the beach playing with the dolphins,
I'm at the beach watching the sunset.

Samantha Antolik (8)
Little Common School

Animals Together

Cat, Cat, chase the mouse,
Right the way through the tree house.
Mouse, Mouse, keep on running for that cheese,
Oh no, here come the honey bees.
Bees, bees guard your honey,
Uh oh, here comes the bunny,
Bunny, Bunny, quickly bounce,
Oh dear, that naughty dog's already given his pounce!
Dog, Dog, fetch the stick,
Fetch it, fetch it, fetch it quick.
And all the animals gather together,
After all, it is such good weather.

Maddie Wilson (7)
Little Common School

The Dragon

From the blood of a human
The monster rose,
With one eye on evil,
The wicked gates close.
His eyes are like flames,
He attacks in the night,
His heart is sable-black
And despises the light.
His eyes are like rubies
Glowing in the dark,
He sleeps all day
In chippings and bark.
His teeth are like razors,
Deadly and keen,
His emerald scales,
Fearsome and mean.

Jenny Smith (11)
Little Common School

Lurking In The Darkness

If you're in the water,
You had better beware,
There are things down in the darkness
That could really give you a scare.
The jellyfish could sting you,
The eels give a nasty bite,
But if a shark is lurking beneath you,
You're in for a terrible fright.
His steely eyes will see you
Swimming up above,
And if he's feeling hungry,
Your leg might feel a tug.

Robert Brighton (8)
Little Common School

Summer

The bright, hot, shimmering sun,
Playing, having
So much fun!

I'm out in the garden
Playing by the pool,
With my stereo,
It's so cool!

Raspberries, strawberries,
Blackcurrants, the best,
They're so delicious,
I gave them to a guest!

Flowers growing,
Grass so green,
Tulips beautiful
As they seem!

Fiona Leggat (9)
Little Common School

Mummy

Dinner server,
Toast maker,
Shopping chatter,
Chocolate eater,
Clothes washer,
TV watcher,
Warm hugger,
Face kisser.

Rebecca Pfaff (7)
Little Common School

Medicine For Grandma

Give me the bladder of a goat,
And an organ from someone's throat,
How about some elephant's ear wax,
And part of a plant called flax?
The heart of a monkey,
The poisonous sting of a scorpion chunky,
A sticky bun
And a baby's bum.
A circus clown (very funny)
And an Egyptian mummy.

'So how do you like it Grandmamma?'
(Snigger, snigger, ha, ha, ha!)
Will it blast you down the road?
Will it make your head overload?
Will it turn you into a toad?
Will you fizz like a can of Coke?
Will you think it's a hoax?
Will it turn you into a frog?
Will you become a chocolate log?
'I hope you like your new medicine Grandma.'

Andrew Slinn (8)
Little Common School

Dolphins

Dolphins glide over the blue blanket of ocean horses,
Their tremendous jaw is as smiley as a camera case,
Dolphins' skin is finer than curtain velvet,
Their eyes are as bright as the sun's blazing flame light,
Their fine fin corners are as round as a thumb nail,
Their long, pointed noses are as elegant as a unicorn in flight,
And that is the wonderful dolphin!

Oscar Hammond (8)
Little Common School

That's What I Wear

A dress and socks
Summer
That's what I wear.

Bikini and goggles
Swimming
That's what I wear.

Purple and black leotard
Gymnastics
That's what I wear.

Jumper, culottes and T-shirt
Brownies
That's what I wear.

Blue leotard, frilly skirt and ballet shoes
Ballet
That's what I wear.

Sparkly dress and high-heeled shoes
Party
That's what I wear.

Beige jacket, green trousers, fishing vest
Fishing
That's what I wear.

Old trousers and old T-shirt
Gardening
That's what I wear.

All-in-one snowsuit
Lapland
That's what I wore when I went to visit Father Christmas last year.

Jodie Henningway (7)
Little Common School

Monsters

When I was running
I definitely saw,
A great big monster,
Then I saw some more.

The monster was
Green and spotty,
His best friend
Is called Dotty.

All his friends
Call him Otter
And sometimes
They call him Spotter.

They like to call him that
Because he sings,
About nice otters
That have got wings.

Dotty's best friend
Is called Hetty,
But she was
Always being called Becky.

Hetty was a good friend
But! She misbehaved
And she never stopped
Talking above caves.

Sophie James (9)
Little Common School

The Sea!

Deep down in the ocean,
Deep under the sea,
There is something
I'd like to see . . .
Sea-blue dolphins,
Fish that can sing.
The sea brings gifts
From faraway lands,
One million diamonds
That glisten in my hand.

Amelia Harrison (9)
Little Common School

Disco

Big shiny disco balls
Turning round and round,
With my fancy dance moves
I'm going to touch the ground,
Get back up again and do it again,
But my head goes all dizzy, it goes all fizzy,
Then the party has to end.
Thank you, I've had a great time,
Your dress really does shine.

Katy Croft (8)
Little Common School

Fireworks

Fireworks, fireworks on fireworks night,
Eating toffee apples all through the night.
There's a *bang* and a *zoom*
And there's sparkles everywhere.
You've got to wrap up warm,
Because it is freezing out there.

Olivia Davies (9)
Little Common School

One Wondrous Washday

Washing machines whirr and whiz!
Hypnotising you with their spinning,
Like a magician swinging a ticking clock.

Pop! Bubbles start exploding.
All types of clothes whirling round and round.
Where will they land?
Which way will they turn?
Where does my missing sock go?

Green, red, blue, orange and yellow,
Multicolours twisting and twirling,
Mashing and mixing.
Chasing each other round and round.
A bubbly loop-the-loop.

The fairground ride ends,
The door goes click.
Plop! Clothes limp and lifeless lay,
Just waiting for another wash day.

Patrick Hills (8)
Little Common School

Australia

The sea is as blue as a summer sky,
The beach is empty, there's not even a fly.
As kangaroos jump,
Their tails go thump.
The sun is so hot and bright,
I think it's time for a water fight.
The kookaburra is perching in his tree,
He just turned round and is looking straight at me!
Paddling in sea foam,
Do I have to go home?

Molly Skelton-Greenwood (9)
Middle Street Primary School

Woky Woky Land

In Woky Woky Land, far, far away,
In the capital, Bong Bar,
In the busy streets of Goffa,
Past the tall tower of Laplap,
In the jungle of Glubglub,
There was a house,
And this house was made of marshmallows.
And in Woky Woky Land, far, far away,
In Bong Bar, in Gaffa, past Laplap, in Glubglub,
Lived the Wocky Wocky in the marshmallow house.
The Wocky Wocky was the first half of a horse,
Head of a snake, neck of a giraffe,
The second half of a zebra, tail of a lion.
The Wocky Wocky was a meanie,
Eating those who dared to enter his marshmallow house/lair.
So one day, a brave man enters the Wocky Wocky's house,
But no lashing pain, so he carried on.
Then the door creaked.
Slash as the man swung his sword.
Smack, smick it went through the neck.
Bang it went on the floor dead, the Wocky Wocky.

Robyn Gall (10)
Middle Street Primary School

Lazy Maisy

There was a girl called Maisy,
She was ever so lazy.
A few years later, she changed to a lady,
And picked a daisy.
The flower in her hand made her prance and prance,
Oh it was so pretty when she decided to dance.

Sienna Gladwin (10)
Middle Street Primary School

The Baggy Girl

There was once a girl called Aggie,
Who only wore baggies,
Then she wore a hood,
No one thought she would,
So she changed her name to Maggie.
She tripped on those baggies
And she lay,
A few years on she was old,
And there she holds
A leaflet about your name being Aggie.

Agnes Vaughan (10)
Middle Street Primary School

Homework, Oh Homework!

Homework, oh homework, I hate you, you stink,
I wish I could wash you away in the sink.
Homework, oh homework, I hate you, I do,
I wish I could flush you down the loo.
Homework, oh homework, you're last on my list,
I don't want to do it, but the teachers insist.
Homework, oh homework, do go away,
You're doing my head in, you cannot stay.

Jasmine Walker (10)
Middle Street Primary School

It's The Half-Term

I am so delighted,
That's why I'm so excited,
Today is the last day of school
And I am going swimming in a big pool.
I don't want to go back to school,
Because I want to go back in that big pool.

Heloise Payne (10)
Middle Street Primary School

Dogs Sleep Anywhere

(Based on 'Cats Sleep Anywhere' by Eleanor Farjean)

Dogs sleep anywhere,
Any dog basket, any sofa,
Top to bottom,
Table leg.
But their favourite
Place to sleep
Is their own mattress!

Lauren Wheeler (10)
Middle Street Primary School

The Man From Mars

There was a man from Mars,
Who was incredibly fast.
When he landed on the moon,
He got caught in a monsoon,
So he got out his umbrella,
This wrinkly old fella,
And slowly died.

Ruby Lewis (10)
Middle Street Primary School

My Baboon

Big baboon sitting on the loo,
Always eating junk food too.
Bananas, burgers, big, fat fries,
Oh he could win the biggest prize.
Only the baboon could not eat this much.
No one could even touch.

Mitchell Mulvay (10)
Middle Street Primary School

McDonald's

I went to McDonald's the other day,
They gave me a tray
Of double cheese burgers, chocolate milk,
Shakes and French fries,
But don't forget the apple pies.
McFlurry's swirling, twirling then
Munch, munch, gobble and slurp
And slurp one more Coke.
I think I'm gonna choke.
With a pop and a fizz and a whizz, 'Yahoo!'
But what I mean, it's only a dream.

Jools Turner (10)
Middle Street Primary School

My Best Friend

My best friend Kizzy,
You can call her Lizzy,
But she's very, very busy,
And she can get dizzy.
Her sister calls her Sissy,
Her mum's called Izzy,
But she's called Kizzy,
Kizzy needs gold.

Daisy Barrell Shearer (9)
Middle Street Primary School

The Crazy Goat

Come on you old goats, get over here now,
Don't get mixed up with that fat cow.
Come on you dog, stop sleeping like a log,
Go fetch that goat that's fishing in the moat.
Come look, she's going mad,
People will think you're very bad . . .

Rosa Steele (9)
Middle Street Primary School

Animals' Medal

Gold flickers flash past.
An eye stares, made of glass.
All the animals head to the temple.
At the top of the jungle heavens,
Animals were called.
The first jungle ever flying
With the pyramid-shaped temple,
Ancient inside, carvings beyond imagination,
Unsleeping eyes, talking mouths,
Shocking neatness, messy hair.
In one person there's a bag of emotion,
A race has been run,
Cheetah won the gold medal.
Antelope came third,
Hare and rabbit came fourth,
Mice fifth and last was Turtle, poor chap,
Old and ancient, but young at 2000!
Gold, silver, bronze, gold-plated,
Stickers and a small kiss for Turtle, and a hug.
A big feast for all who take part,
Then the big party with everyone.
The new day, a new race for everyone!
And yet again shocking news, Turtle won!
A big cheer, clapping like mad.
Turtle is amazing.
Five cheers for turtle.

Poppy Gandy (10)
Middle Street Primary School

The Magic Chocolate Bar

Joey the magic chocolate bar lives in a pub,
They only serve drinks and not never grub.
On a plate with his wand
He can make chocolate.

Declan Hall (10)
Middle Street Primary School

Words Of The Snowmen

'Spring is coming, the end is near, oh help!'
Say the snowmen, can you hear?
You know it's apocalypse?
It's all the sun's fault!
The snowmen are screaming,
'Oh no, we're melting, oh no.
If only we weren't all made out of snow!
What was the purpose of our creation?
Oh this melting, what tarnation!'
All over England snowmen are wilting,
Even King Snowman is tilting.
Spring is here, we're waiting, daffodils,
All the snow has cleared from the hills.
Now everybody has forgotten the snowmen's cries,
They're all looking forward to deep blue skies.

Myles Keep-Stothard (10)
Middle Street Primary School

I Smell A Rat!

There was a rat who lived under the stairs,
Who nibbled things like apples and pears.
He scampered around without a sound,
He teased the cat, would you fancy that?
He has decided to stay to this very day.

Ivy Klein (10)
Middle Street Primary School

Animals

Tigers roaring in the wild,
Kittens playing like a child.
Dogs barking at each other,
Puppies drinking from their mother.

Tazmin Barton (10)
Ninfield CE Primary School

Haunted House

I stepped inside the abandoned mansion,
The door creaked open,
Into the darkness I walked,
I turned on the camcorder and light,
Slowly I crept across the old dusty floorboards,
Then up the stairs, filming every second.
Into an empty room I crept,
Then the door shut.
I jumped around and heard a creak from behind me.
Slowly I turned around,
Then I saw a cradle rock.
Suddenly a ghost appeared from behind a bed,
Then I realised it didn't have a head.
From then I ran and ran,
Until I saw my gran.

Ben Jones (11)
Ninfield CE Primary School

Teachers

Teachers, I hate them so much.
They make me lose my perfect touch.
They're howling at me all the time,
Expecting me to be on question 9.
It's really unfair how they howl at me,
Why can't they just howl at Becky?
I really hate teachers, do you know why?
Because they make me think
About homework all through the night.
But you must admit, some teachers are actually nice.

Matthew Broadbent (9)
Ninfield CE Primary School

Why Are Teachers So Bossy?

I've always wondered why teachers are so bossy,
Whilst I looked through the window daydreaming,
'Why aren't you paying attention?' the teacher said.
'Sorry!' I said, not meaning it.
One time they say take your time, take your time,
The next, they go, 'Why aren't you on question five?'
To be honest they switch off, not us!

I've always wondered what's in a teacher's brain.
I imagine them as a robot with stiff arms and legs.
They get controlled by aliens, that's who they take after!
What is your teacher like?
All of our school has women teachers
And a woman headmistress too.
We've had a big change, our old teacher is
Now our headmistress!
In half a term, we have a new teacher called Mr Sandaver.
I still have one year and five months
Until I go to High school. I can't wait!

Sarah Campbell (10)
Ninfield CE Primary School

The Walk

I went down the path and what did I see?
I saw a monkey climbing a tree.

I went down the path and what did I see?
I saw an ant crawling up my knee.

I went down the path and what did I see?
I saw a bee looking at me.

James Godden (10)
Ninfield CE Primary School

Cats

Pouncing, leaping, crawling, sleeping,
Cats, cats,
Catching, chasing, eating, drinking,
Cats, cats,
Looking, spotting, eating, drinking,
Cats, cats,
Finding, thinking, wondering, seeing,
Cats, cats.

Hannah Caney (11)
Ninfield CE Primary School

The Sky

The sky is like a big face,
Its hair is the fluffy clouds,
Its eyes and mouth are the blue spaces.
The face looks down on me.
When it is hot, it breathes its hot breath,
When it is cold, it breathes its icy-cold breath.
This face will forever stay with me.

Tabitha Hilton-Berry (10)
Ninfield CE Primary School

Horses

H orses are lovely! Horses are nice!
   have a go on them, have a try.
O n a horse you're up in the air feeling giddy.
R eins are steady, reins hold you tight.
S teady and slow they sometimes go.
E xaggerate your hair, exaggerate your body, feel calm.
S uper horses, super food, have a go and toot your hoot!

Sophie Connor (9)
Ninfield CE Primary School

Walking In The Jungle

Who would want to walk in the jungle?
Who'd want to walk with me
And meet the shaggy, baggy flotsam tigers
In the jungle?

Who would want to walk in the jungle?
Who'd want to walk with me
And meet the slithery snakes in the jungle?

Who would want to walk in the jungle?
Who'd want to walk with me
And meet the beautiful coloured toucan
Parrot in the jungle?

Who would want to walk in the jungle?
Who'd want to walk with me
And meet the vicious, snappy, flappy crock
In the jungle?

Alice Smith (10)
Ninfield CE Primary School

My Teacher

Teachers are very grumpy,
All through their lives,
(Trust me!)
I mean,
Take it from me,
There is only one teacher as nice as mine
In the whole word,
Mrs Smith,
She is so kind.
(Even though she gives us lots of homework!)
Fairly easy work and lots of fun!
And giggles!

Harriet Sinfoil (10)
Ninfield CE Primary School

Teachers

We like to play,
But the teacher's don't.
And we always have to answer a question at a certain time.
They don't bother helping us
When we're stuck,
So what do you get?
Yell, yell, yell!
We have loads of homework,
My brother doesn't get as much.
Me and my class
Find the lessons *boring!*
So we start talking.
Teachers must go off in a daydream or be deaf,
Because they don't hear us (that's good.)
I don't understand, they sit on their bums
And write reports,
And at the end of the year,
We get bad *remarks!*

Abbie Ballard (10)
Ninfield CE Primary School

My Exploration In The Jungle

I went into the jungle and guess what I saw?
A massive lion going, 'Roar, roar, roar.'
Then I turned around and I saw a great croc,
I ran away in surprise and shock.
As I ran away, I heard a big bang,
And in the tree I saw an orang-utan.
I look around and next I see
A great gorilla chasing after me.
Then I saw a massive lake,
In it was an anaconda snake.

Ryan Allen (11)
Ninfield CE Primary School

The Days Tick By

The night ticks by,
I'm asleep.
The night ticks by with a freak.
I'm in the bed fast asleep,
Aah, this is scary.

Lessons tick by slowly,
This is boring.
Lessons tick by slowly, like on a plane.
Life is like a daydream.

Leanne Newnham (11)
Ninfield CE Primary School

Kittens

Kittens are cute,
And so's my newt.
My dad hates them,
But I love them.
I don't know why,
He'd hit them between the eyes,
But dads are dads,
And we can't change that.

Anna Saxby Foster (9)
Ninfield CE Primary School

Homework

H orrible,
O ld,
M ean,
E vil,
W ormish,
O gre,
R otten,
K ilt.

Alexander Mitchell (10)
Ninfield CE Primary School

The Chase

I looked through the bush
And what did I see?
A spider chasing me.

I looked through the bush
And what did I see?
Snakes wriggling after me.

I looked through the bush
And what did I see?
Scorpions snapping at me.

I looked through the bush
And what did I see?
Mosquitoes darting towards me.

Harry Saunders (10)
Ninfield CE Primary School

My Teacher

There are many monkeys in our school,
Not the children - but our teachers.
They climb to the top of the tower,
They could see some reachers.
Monkeys are my teachers,
Sometimes they are jolly and sometimes mad.

Adam Franks (11)
Ninfield CE Primary School

Haiku

I swung on the swing
with Nathan and Samuel.
Sam fell off the swing.

Charlie Bennett (10)
Patcham House Special School

Haiku

The acorn was hard.
We pushed it into a box.
An oak tree will grow.

Nathan Lovegrove (10)
Patcham House Special School

Haiku

We saw rabbit holes,
They were round and looked quite cosy.
Are rabbits furry?

Jack Wright (10)
Patcham House Special School

Haiku

The dog was lovely.
It was smell and quite big.
He ran first to me.

Dave Upton (9)
Patcham House Special School

Haiku

We pushed the wheelbarrow.
Susan helped dig up the leaves.
The worms are slimy.

Michael Patrick (8)
Patcham House Special School

Haiku

We were getting worms.
They felt slimy and sticky.
They were slow and wet.

Kelly Gunn (10)
Patcham House Special School

Haiku

The dog was funny.
He felt hairy and fluffy.
He was named Stacker.

Sam Humphrey (11)
Patcham House Special School

Green

Green are the trees
that wave in the breeze.

Green are the cats' eyes
that stare in the night.

Green are buildings found
deep in the countryside.

Green are the peas and broccoli
found on my plate.

Green are the army
who fight for our country.

Green are the leaves and grass
that help to make up the earth.

Green are the aliens
that live on other planets.

Aston Peters (8)
St Aubyns School, Brighton

Pirate Jack

Pirate Jack was a nasty guy,
A man of sixty-four,
An eye-patch and a bloodshot eye,
And a knack for defying the law.

Climbing up the rigging,
Shouting on the deck,
Many ships a-sailing,
Reduced to a burning wreck.

Hairy Sam, the second mate,
Another lad or two,
Ran the deathly destiny,
A truly terrifying crew.

Gold and silver pistols,
Clunking on his belt,
How on earth did he survive so long,
The way that Sam smelt?

But Pirate Jack is deceased now,
Along with Hairy Sam,
And now I will just tell you how:
There was poison in his jam.

Hugh Jeffery (11)
St Aubyns School, Brighton

Colours

Red is a rose so pure.
Black is like a cat's gaze.
Yellow is as happy as a sun.
Green is like Mother Nature blooming.
Purple is as delicate as a plum.
Blue is free like the sea.
Pink is as beautiful as a girl.
Grey is as strong as an elephant.

Aimee Barron (10)
St Aubyns School, Brighton

Colours

Colours, colours everywhere
Blue, purple and red
I love colours
They're everywhere

The bottom of the sea is blue
Like the top of the sky

The sun is red
Like the roses
On Valentine's Day

Giving chocolates
I love chocolates
But I hate brown

I like colours!

Jessica Poulter (8)
St Aubyns School, Brighton

Sun

Hot, light, very
bright. Do not look at it,
it damages sight. I love you
sun, you make plants grow. You do us
favours and help farmers sow. I love you
sun, you give us good light. You're up in
the morning and gone in the night.
I love you sun, you give us good
heat, you're up in the morning
and gone when
we sleep.

Timmy Calliafas (8)
St Aubyns School, Brighton

Mother

Her eyes are like two spongy buns,
Her nose is like a soft brown drum,
Her mouth is like a bright half moon,
Her teeth are like squares of silver coconut,
Her voice is like a smooth blue sea,
Her ears are like a half-shaped ball,
Her chin is like a warm, silk quilt,
Her hands are like a bumpy road,
Her hair is like a flowing waterfall,
Her head is like a golden locket.

Riya Nambiar (7)
St Bede's Prep School, Eastbourne

My Twin Brother

His eyes are like two wheels on a motorbike,
His nose is like a squishy banana,
His mouth is like an apple on a tree,
His ears are like soft bunny rabbits' ears,
His teeth are like George Washington's wooden teeth,
His chin is like a pink planet,
His hands are like the hairy paw of a fox,
His hair is like a mop standing on its end,
His head is like a baby rugby ball.

Jamie Whelan (8)
St Bede's Prep School, Eastbourne

My Dad

His eyes are like deep pools of bluebells.
His nose is like a soft peach,
His mouth is like an old ticking grandfather clock,
His chin is like an owl's beak,
His arms are like two skinny chips.

Georgia Mae Ellis (8)
St Bede's Prep School, Eastbourne

Daddy

His eyes are like two brown spheres,
His nose is like a cold pink sausage,
His mouth is like a pink sponge,
His legs are like two skinny baguettes,
His hair is like a black hairbrush,
His fingers are like tubes of strip lighting,
His body is like a pizza with cheese,
His voice is like a rough sea,
His arms are like cement cylinders,
His hands are like a burger with salad oozing out.

Jordan Thomas (7)
St Bede's Prep School, Eastbourne

My Daddy

His eyes are like two square clocks,
His nose is like a tasty hot dog,
His mouth is like a telephone,
His feet are like a pair of scissors,
His head is like a red tulip tree,
His body is like a rubber rectangle,
His ears are like door handles.

Gheorghe Richards (9)
St Bede's Prep School, Eastbourne

My Brother Michael

His eyes are like the spring bluebells,
His nose is like a sloping hill,
His mouth is like two bent flowers,
His feet are like long rulers,
His head is like an Easter egg,
His arms are like a pair of wings.

Abigail Quinn (7)
St Bede's Prep School, Eastbourne

Have You Ever

Have you ever seen a table with long, rocky legs?
Have you ever seen a washing line with green, mossy pegs?
Have you ever seen a building with ears on the roof?
Have you ever seen a man with a shiny, golden tooth?

Have you ever seen the Queen's knickers really up close?
Have you ever seen Tony Blair pick his nose?
Have you ever seen Britney Spears with your hose?
Have you ever been on the Saturday Show?

Have you ever been sick on a roller coaster?
Have you ever been shoved in your granny's toaster?
Have you ever knocked out your village's grocer?
Have you ever been known as a marshmallow roaster?

Have you ever gone fishing and caught a toad?
Have you ever carried an ultra heavy load?
Have you ever been in high hyper mode?
Have you ever found out what is a goad?

I have.

Henry Miller (8)
St Bede's Prep School, Eastbourne

Sandstorm In A Football Stadium

It was a hot day in Asia, then the heard a noise in the stadium.

The sandstorm leapt over the stadium and crushed all the seats
and then all the sand went flying and trampled the people.

The sand sprinted towards the players who whooshed
through the doors.

It battered the stadium to pieces and forced the players
to scamper away.
The sandstorm flung sand into the eyes of everyone and blinded them.

Oliver Tingley (9)
St Bede's Prep School, Eastbourne

Writing By Torchlight

Is somebody there?
Who made that noise?
What was that?
Can they hear me?
Who closed the cupboard?
Who moved the chair?
Who flushed the chain?
What was that noise?
Do they know what I'm doing?
Here my parents come,
Boy, am I in trouble.

Can't write by torchlight now,
They've confiscated my torch,
Grounded for two weeks as well,
But I still write at night,
Just borrow my sister's mobile,
The light's enough at night.

I wonder if they did hear me?
Or, did you tell them?
No?
Then I bet it was my sister!

Eleanor James (10)
St Bede's Prep School, Eastbourne

Dropping Stuff

Ever dropped a baby out a window? Agoooo, smash
Ever dropped a cow out of ten-story flat? Moooooo, kasplat
Ever dropped a dog out an aeroplane over water? Wooooo, splash
Ever dropped your best friend off a roof? Heeellpp! Whack, I don't like
you anymore.
Ever dropped a clock from your room to the floor? Tick-tock, tick
tock tock.

Nick Salway (9)
St Bede's Prep School, Eastbourne

Tidal Wave In A City

The tidal wave leapt into the city
And destroyed everything in its path.

It buried the city in water
And drowned the buildings.

It took down a skyscraper
In one blast of water.

Waves pouncing and tumbling
Smashing the city to pieces.

It swallowed lorries and cars
As though they were chocolate bars.

The waves swirled and whirled
Making the city into a washing machine.

As the waves stopped spinning
The survivors stared at their smashed homes.

Harry Devall (8)
St Bede's Prep School, Eastbourne

Volcano On A Mountain

The volcano erupted all of a sudden
It spurted out of the mountain

The river of lava twisted and turned
Flowing through the trees

Lurching, zooming, rushing, whizzing
Covering all in its path

People were screaming, scrambling for life
Diving into a nearby pool of water

The lava destroyed houses in the village
And covered every living thing.

Timothy Fielding (8)
St Bede's Prep School, Eastbourne

Hospital

Nee naw, nee naw,
Who's that coming through the door?
Oh no, it's a boy,
His arm is lying on the floor.
Call a doctor, get some thread,
Tie him down onto a bed.
Give him some pills to kill the pain,
Then stitch the arm back on again.
Then at last when all is done,
Send him home with his mum.

Mark Ramesar (9)
St Bede's Prep School, Eastbourne

My Cat Ben

My cat Ben sat on a pen, which squirted ink on the floor,
I slipped on the ink, which led to the sink next door,
He ran outside, slipped on a slide and fell on his backside on a core,
He jumped in the air, walked in his lair to find a rat on the floor.

Adam Elliott (9)
St Bede's Prep School, Eastbourne

Poems

Poems - they can be . . .
Funny, sad, boring, interesting,
Good, bad, silly, weird.
But most of all . . .
They're hard to write.
So when you read a bad poem
Never say it's bad because
You never know how hard
Someone's worked on it.

Barbara Roberts (9)
St Bede's Prep School, Eastbourne

My Dad

His eyes are like two brown chocolate pies,
His nose is like a sloping, icy mountain,
His mouth is like red shiny cherries,
His hair is like a field of cut grass,
His ears are like curly pigs' tails,
His arms are like a big, overgrown jungle,
His back is like a strong, flat tabletop,
His teeth are like white, round pearls,
His feet are like cocoa-coloured hairy spiders,
His chin is like a rough piece of sandpaper.

Ayesha Mitchell (8)
St Bede's Prep School, Eastbourne

The Fly

To the fly a wasp is a cruel leopard
A cereal box is Mount Everest to him
The red rose's thorn is as sharp as a spear
And raindrops are like fierce bullets
A human to the fly is a Twin Tower
And a daisy's petals are like a feather bed
The world can be vicious to the fly
But the fly gets its own back on the world.

Cary Frame (9)
St Bede's Prep School, Eastbourne

The Moon

The moon is like a pearl
On a lush, velvet background,
With diamonds everywhere
And marbles all in a circle,
Going around a big orange cat in the middle,
Curled up in a ball.

Mona Darabi-Fard (9)
St Bede's Prep School, Eastbourne

A Laugh Of Limericks

There was a young girl from Spain
Whose head got stuck down the drain
She tried yelling for help
But out came a yelp
She now sticks to driving a train.

There was a young girl from Greece
Who wanted to bring the world peace
She started at France
And learnt a new dance
She then changed her name to Clarrice.

There was a blue alien from Mars
Who decided to buy eighteen cars
He was caught in a crash
And got a big bash
He now sticks to watching the stars.

There was a young boy from France
Who unexpectedly got in a trance
He brought yellow cream
To help his weird dream
And decided to learn a long dance.

There was a young boy from Peru
Who wanted to go to the zoo
He got in a fight
And got a big bite
And now he can't do anything but chew.

Charlotte Davidson (10)
St Bede's Prep School, Eastbourne

School

The school is not cool,
It's home that will rule,
Cos of the PlayStation 2,
And the TVs and all!

Chayton Kent (9)
St Bede's Prep School, Eastbourne

The Sea

A cliff breaker,
A stone masher,
A wave maker,
A monster breeder,
A ship wrecker,
A raging tiger,
A quiet, old mouse,
A fishes' house,
The animals' shopping centre,
Always on the move.

William Denning (10)
St Bede's Prep School, Eastbourne

Cinquain

Night-time
When will it go?
I want it to be day.
Now that day is here go
Away evening.

Alexandra Steel (9)
St Bede's Prep School, Eastbourne

Car

A road whizzer.
A door slammer.
A seat sitter.
A shopping bag holder.
An engine roarer.
A wheel spinner.
A sunroof flipper.

Guy Clarke (10)
St Bede's Prep School, Eastbourne

Daylight

Daylight
Shining bright sky
With a blazing, big sun
A nice curtain of glowing light
Sky bright.

Toby Copeland (8)
St Bede's Prep School, Eastbourne

Daylight

Daylight
blazing so bright
in dawn spreading colours
with the clouds passing by
birds sing.

Naomi Dowse (9)
St Bede's Prep School, Eastbourne

Daylight

Daylight
Beautiful light
A nice display to watch
A great hot sphere in a bright sky
Shine bright.

Chloe Parker (8)
St Bede's Prep School, Eastbourne

Snowflakes

Snowflakes fall softly
The beautiful snowflakes
Swiftly through the air.

Amelia Goldman (8)
St Bede's Prep School, Eastbourne

My Hamster

My hamster called Peaches
Has eyes like glowing red traffic lights
A nose like pale pink ham
Little white whiskers like optic fibres
Silky, soft fur the colours of peaches and cream
Minute, delicate little paws like little fingers
Which she uses to carefully nibble her food
Long, sharp teeth are like a pitchfork
A tiny, short, hairy tail like pink wire
Big, fat pouches like hot air balloons
She swings from her cage bars
Like a monkey does through the trees.

George Hayward (8)
St Bede's Prep School, Eastbourne

Night Poem

The darkness of the night
might give you a fright.
When you pull the blind down
the creatures surely frown.
Not the owl,
it can see in the dark clearly.
Shapeless creatures approach you.
That's when you wonder
who is out there looking in at *you!*

Gregory Paxton (8)
St Bede's Prep School, Eastbourne

Daylight

Look at the sun
The sun appears above the sea
Like half bitten semi-circle
Good morning.

Sidony Taylor (8)
St Bede's Prep School, Eastbourne

A Tree

When a tree starts to grow,
It will be very small,
But before you know,
It has grown quite tall.

So don't you think,
When you see a tree,
That that is how,
It will always be.

A tree will never be the same,
Until it is reborn again.

Harry Joe Potter (7)
St Bede's Prep School, Eastbourne

When My Mum's Away

Next week my mum's away,
So my friends can come to play.
We'll play a game of Twister,
But not my baby sister.
My brother he might play,
But, he'll have to pay.
We'll have a day of fun,
Playing in the sun.

Lloyd Heathfield (7)
St Bede's Prep School, Eastbourne

Daylight

Daylight
Sunlight shining
A glowing, sunny face
And a big and sunny smile.

Matthew Freeman (8)
St Bede's Prep School, Eastbourne

I Can Fly

I believe I can fly away
right the way to the USA.

I believe I can fly away
right the way over the Milky Way.

I'll fly so high
with the birds in the sky.

I'll fly over mountains
and meet up with fountains.

Then I'll land on the sand
and play with the band.

And then I'll go home
to my bubble bath foam.

James Hammond (8)
St Bede's Prep School, Eastbourne

Tornado In A Village

The tornado rushed through the village
And whizzed along the roads.

The people got swooped up by the win,
And all the animals too.

The roof tiles were flying to and fro.
Some were bashing into car windows.

It sucked the windows out of their sockets
Leaving glass slices in branches.

People were darting and tumbling down the road
Scampering for their lives.

Daniel Wells (8)
St Bede's Prep School, Eastbourne

Fireworks

Fireworks are bright
Fireworks are beautiful
Fireworks are loud
They make a great big sound.

They fizz and pop
And whirl and twirl
And sizzle and sparkle
And swirl and curl.

They bang and burn
And spin and spit
And crack and shoot
And whoosh and flit.

Charlie Price (7)
St Bede's Prep School, Eastbourne

The Planet

I saw an orange planet
It was a strange looking planet
I went there in my spaceship
But then it turned to red

It was very, very cold
With wrinkles and spots
But I had a look around
And saw a little cave

Inside there was an alien
With lots of eyes
So I flew back home
To my cosy bed.

Calum Robertson (7)
St Bede's Prep School, Eastbourne

The Sky

I am your nightmare
When it's time for bed.
And even though I'm pretty
I'm lurking in your head.
My shooting stars are shining bright,
Why are you hiding away?
Why don't you make a wish tonight
And then come out to play?

Daniel Drewek (7)
St Bede's Prep School, Eastbourne

Saturday

S aturday is my best day
A ll my friends come over to play
T hey play cards and crazy bones
U nder the tree
R acing and 'it'
D ecided to play the games you want
A tree to climb
Y es Saturday is my best day.

Ben Howell (8)
St Bede's Prep School, Eastbourne

Autumn

A ll the leaves are turning brown
U nder the trees there are heaps of leaves
T aking the leaves from the trees is the wind
U nder the trees then the wind is blowing
M any leaves are on the ground
N one of the leaves are on the trees.

Christopher Pearce (8)
St Bede's Prep School, Eastbourne

Rhyming Food

Hey dinner lady, who likes what?
Well there's Rod,
He likes cod.
And there's Grace,
She likes plaice.
But Pete . . . well,
He likes meat.
What kind of meat?
He's not fussy.
Where as Billy,
She'll only eat chilli.
And Murray,
He'll only eat curry.
What about Tony?
He eats macaroni.
And there's Lurkey,
He eats turkey.
Lurkey?
Who on earth is Lurkey?
We'll he big and fat,
He's the school cat.
OK then, so what about David?
He eats erm . . .
He goes home for dinner.

David Edwards (9)
St Bede's Prep School, Eastbourne

A Hurricane In A Village

It came skidding to the village crushing houses.
Roofs flung through the air, windmills spinning making flour.
It went whizzing, destroying half a barn, wood tossed to and fro.
Digging a thick ditch it zoomed on from the half barn.
As it dashed to its next target, it left a breeze trotting in the park.

Ted Willis-Slater (9)
St Bede's Prep School, Eastbourne

What Am I?

An upside down-sleeper
A fast-flyer
A fly-chaser
A night-watcher
A sharp-biter
A fruit-eater
A cave-liver
A fur-wearer
A milk-drinker
A blind-looker
A midnight-worker
A loud-screamer
A day-dreamer.

Joel Robson Lambourne (9)
St Bede's Prep School, Eastbourne

What Am I?

A big-mouth.
A fish-eater.
A sea-liver.
A people-scarer.
A fast-swimmer.
A quiet-mover.
A scent-hunter.
A water-hunter.
A sharp-tooth.
A grey-skin.

James Moody (9)
St Bede's Prep School, Eastbourne

Kenning

A stone cruncher
A blue gobbler
A big drowner
A salt muncher
A big dipper
A huge floater
A cold shower
A fish tank
A land swamper
A dangerous wrecker.

What am I?

(The sea).

Bethany Bagnall (8)
St Bede's Prep School, Eastbourne

Cheetah Kenning

A rocket-racer
A jungle-runner
A spot-nicker
A meat-hunter
A water-lapper
A tree-hugger
A stealth-king
A feast-prowler
A loner-roamer.

Andrew Brundle (9)
St Bede's Prep School, Eastbourne

Rain On A Boat

The rain crashed and slammed into the boat,
the rain splattered down against the wood.

People skidded around, falling off the boat,
whizzing, zooming down into the waves.

Waves shooting up and shooting down, foam spraying,
cracking against the boat and zooming in.

Sails were flapping while people tried
to get the sails down.

People trying not to cry but they go out into the waves
praying they would survive.

Amy Rimmington (8)
St Bede's Prep School, Eastbourne

Hail On A Boat

The hail was smashing the window
and was rolling about the boat.

The people were rushing over the boat
and swimming to shore.

The boat crashed into the lighthouse
and the light tumbled into the sea.

The boat sank to the bottom of the sea
and was crushed to smithereens.

The hail was pounding on the sailors' heads
while they were trying to flee to safety.

Jonah Winterton (8)
St Bede's Prep School, Eastbourne

The Wind And Its Voices

Every time when I lay in bed,
I think about what the story said.

The wind whistles through the night
With just the deepest moonlight,
It sounds like a wolf howling out
And then a child walking about.

Then I hear a lion roar,
With a flash of lightning that just soars,
All of a sudden a scream I hear,
I see a little ghostly tear.

'What's your name?' I asked her twice,
An awkward silence she petted her mice.
Intimidated by the expression,
After that I'd learnt my lesson.

Then I woke up,
It was all a dream!
I dreamt it all,
There was no scream.

I listened hard to the wind next night,
It was just making scary noises,
The things now that I'll never forget,
Were the extremely scary, frightening voices . . .

Crystal Rodrigues (10)
St Mary's C Primary School, Brighton

Lion

Deep, deep down in the lands of Africa,
The lion lays under an old tree.
You go trembling past, hoping he won't pounce,
But he is chasing after you, catching you,
Then eating you for dinner.
So, he's sure to get you, so . . .
Beware!

Phoebe Thorpe (10)
St Mary's C Primary School, Brighton

A Soft Day

Above the sea, in the cloudy sky,
All different kinds of birds fly high,
But in the sea beneath the waves,
Crabs are scuttling into caves.

Mist hangs in the damp, wet air,
A fox hides in his burrowed lair.
A hedgehog's found curled in a ball,
Swifts swoop up, then neatly fall.

It starts to pour with hail and rain,
Some farmers finish cutting grain.
Inside the house the fire burns bright,
The cat sleeps near its flickering light!

It slowly changes from rain to snow,
Across the land the fun will grow.
Children's faces show delight,
They're going to sledge all through the night!

Rhiannon Haestier (10)
St Mary's C Primary School, Brighton

My Little Sister

I love my little sister
But she is such a pain
She messes up our bedroom
And throws my dollies down the drain
She once cut Barbie's hair off
And put Ken in a dress!
She painted all over our bedroom wall
And made a terrible mess
When Mummy saw what she had done
She said that she could weep
But I love my little sister, especially
When she's asleep!

Shush!

Eleanor Dowds (8)
St Mary's C Primary School, Brighton

The Firework Night

Hooray, hooray, it's the firework night,
There's lots of colours, beautiful and bright.
My dad is really happy,
I am full of joy,
My mum is excited,
While my sister plays with a toy.
The bonfire is blazing,
Hot and shining bright,
But when the fireworks start,
My sister jumps in fright.

Henry Groenen (8)
St Mary's RC Primary School, Crowborough

To Belong

To be in a family takes lots of time and care,
Daddy sometimes gets angry, he's started to lose his hair.
When you see a happy family it brings a smile to your face,
When you see a broken family your heart quickens in pace.
Homes hide you from the badness in the world,
You can run to your room, and lie down tightly curled.

Dominique Ollivier (9)
St Mary's RC Primary School, Crowborough

Arctic Weather

It was so cold
That I felt my skin peel away
And frostbite take control of me

It was *so extreme*
I could feel the cold air around me
Like glitter.

Peter Spyrka (8)
St Mary's RC Primary School, Crowborough

My Family Poem

We visit our family in Liverpool
We have lots of fun, it's really cool
We stay at Nana's at Christmas time
We sometimes watch a pantomime
I go to stay with my uncle Paul
He takes me out to play football
My birthday is on 16th December
I get lots of presents when people remember.

Bradley Goldsmith (9)
St Mary's RC Primary School, Crowborough

My Family

I feel happy when I'm at home,
I never feel sad, upset or alone.
When I need help, or when I'm in trouble,
My family will be there at the double.
When I am sick, cold or ill,
I know that my family will be there still.
They always seem to be right there,
And I know that they will always care.

Joe Hicks (9)
St Mary's RC Primary School, Crowborough

Times At Home

When I climb into my bed,
All things are going round in my head.
And as the moon and stars are shining bright,
They fill my room with glowing light.
When we are eating Sunday roasts,
It's time like these I love the most,
Because when my family are together,
It makes me want it to last forever.

Rebecca Hawkins (8)
St Mary's RC Primary School, Crowborough

Family Birthdays

My family's birthdays are such fun,
And they come along one by one.

First it's my dad, it's in June,
And he says forty has come too soon.

Next it's my mum, it's in July,
If you ask her age she'll only lie.

Then in August I was eight,
So now I'm allowed to stay up late.

My sister was six in September,
And she keeps telling me so I remember.

That was my family's birthdays one by one,
To open cards and presents is great fun.

Connor Plane (8)
St Mary's RC Primary School, Crowborough

Family Fun

Playing in the garden,
Having lots of fun,
Along comes little brother,
Running in the sun.

Going out to dinner,
Mum and Dad come too,
Off to our favourite place,
There's always something new.

Along comes night,
Snuggle up tight,
I do love my bed,
'Night to my favourite ted.

Victoria Huxley (9)
St Mary's RC Primary School, Crowborough

Family Times

Every year around July way,
We always have a family day.
Every Christmas we have a nice ham,
It makes a change from bread and jam.
Every New Year we stay up late,
With my mum's friend Kate.
Every birthday it comes and does,
Where time goes, no one knows.
Every Sunday we have roast,
That's the thing I like the most.

Tom Nicoll (9)
St Mary's RC Primary School, Crow

My Family

My family is a treasure,
A gold and shining box,
Filled with love and happiness,
A family I can trust.

I love my family dearly,
It's like my very best friend,
My family is always honest,
On them I can depend.

Wren Lane (9)
St Mary's RC Primary School, Crowborough

Christmas Day At Home

It's Christmas day, hooray, hooray!
My family is happy, so am I.
It's really exciting, I'll tell you why,
There are presents on the floor, and some near the door.
I'm so happy it's Christmas day,
I love it so much, hooray, hooray!

Holly Barrett (9)
St Mary's RC Primary School, Crowborough

In Our Family

Family traditions we have a few,
Christmas time and Easter too.
It all goes back to a country far away,
It's Poland and it is here to stay.
Christmas Eve we all sit to eat,
A fabulous feast but not one bit of meat.
For Easter time we paint those eggs,
And then a basket we all decorate.
For Easter Monday we celebrate that spring is in the air,
We all lie around in wait and sprinkle water everywhere.

Karolina Chalk (9)
St Mary's RC Primary School, Crowborough

Fireworks

Lovely fireworks shining bright,
Then at home we say goodnight.
In the morning we have toast,
My sister likes spaghetti the most,
But I think nuggets are the best.
My birthday and Christmas will soon be here,
In Sussex, for the first time this year.
Nine candles on my cake there will be,
And there will be a great Christmas tree.

Joseph Reidy (9)
St Mary's RC Primary School, Crowborough

My House

I live in a house with my mum and dad,
We are moving soon and it makes me quite sad.

I will miss my friends and the neighbours too,
But new friends I'll make, I'll bet I do.

Henry Garrett (8)
St Mary's RC Primary School, Crowborough

Footballers

Footballers, footballers everywhere,
You see them here, you see them there.
You see them at the stadium when they're playing well,
When they score it makes you shout and yell.

Footballers, footballers everywhere,
When you see them they're very rare.
They laugh about with other men,
And sign autographs with their favourite pen.

Harry Dobson (9)
St Mary's RC Primary School, Crowborough

Go And Open The Door

Go and open the door
You could see . . .
The Mad Hatter running from Scooby Doo
Go and open the door
Oh, what is it?
It's a ghost of the wolf of Toyland.
Go and open the door
Perhaps you'll see
A skeleton on the lawn singing songs.
Are you brave enough to open the door?

Ethan Martyn (7)
St Peter And St Paul Primary School, Bexhill-on-Sea

Through That Door

Through that door is treasure land
Where dragons live
And gold coins are buried
Deep beneath the sand.

Arran Blows (8)
St Peter And St Paul Primary School, Bexhill-on-Sea

Go And Open The Door

Go and open the door
Perhaps you'll see
People walking on the path
Or your friends riding their bikes
Or maybe you'll see
A fire-breathing dragon with fire spitting in your face
Or a flying spaceship
But don't be afraid
Go and open the door

Go and open the door
Perhaps you'll hear
Cars travelling along the road
Or wind whistling through the trees
Or maybe you'll hear
A boxing kangaroo - it's trying to punch you
The roaring of bears surrounding your garden
But don't be afraid
Go and open the door!

Oliver Woodward (8)
St Peter And St Paul Primary School, Bexhill-on-Sea

Go And Open The Door . . .

Go and open the door
Perhaps you'll see

A cat purring on the doorstep
A newspaper boy delivering the morning paper

Or maybe you'll see

A teddy bear playing hopscotch in the garden
A jumping alien

But don't be afraid
Go and open the door.

Amy Webb (7)
St Peter And St Paul Primary School, Bexhill-on-Sea

Beyond The Doorway

Through that door I see
Treasure Land
With lots of mermaids
And pirates searching for treasure.
I see
A beautiful, golden castle
And a pretty princess going to a monster's wedding.
I see and I feel the wind.
I see a monster going to a football match - but they didn't let him in.
I see a vampire jumping up and down.
I hear a monster crying in his cave - so sad and lonely.
I hear mermaids singing so prettily.
I see a mum watching over a vampire that has hurt his leg very badly.
I see a peaceful land of unicorns and flowers and beauty.
Look beyond the doorway
What can you see?

Rachelle Diedericks (7)
St Peter And St Paul Primary School, Bexhill-on-Sea

Go And Open The Door . . .

Go and open the door
Perhaps you'll see

The BBC news people on your doorstep
Waiting to take your photo

Or maybe you'll see

A vampire on the roof, dressed as Santa
Stuffing a green, fire-breathing dragon down the chimney!

But don't be afraid
Go and open the door.

Jem Lewis (8)
St Peter And St Paul Primary School, Bexhill-on-Sea

The Monster's Tail

The creepy, crawly monster
Comes to your house,
Giving you terrifying nightmares
That will keep you up for life.
Going into your room,
Giving you messages writing in blood . . .
Until the night you stay awake
And see the creepy crawly monster
Coming to scare you . . .
The next night the monster does not come,
You terrified the monster,
You gave him a fright.
At breakfast
Out of the window you see
The monster turning to shreds.
And that's the last you'll ever see
Of the creepy, crawly monster.
Sleep tight!

Georgina Marston (8)
St Peter And St Paul Primary School, Bexhill-on-Sea

The House Of Horrors

Enter the House of Horrors
And see what is living in the gloom.
Look a skeleton playing chess
I didn't know that's what he did to rest!
Through the next door and into the loo
Is a ghost complaining about his underwear
I don't want to go in there!
In the next room - a fat vampire
Stand back and run.
He is going to do the biggest burp ever -
Burp, done!
Argh!

Daniel McKenna (8)
St Peter And St Paul Primary School, Bexhill-on-Sea

Through That Door . . .

Through that door
Manchester United V Batman and Robin
Awake for kick-off at Old Trafford.
Two minutes to go,
The crowd are going mad.
And they're off.
Manchester United have the ball,
Here's Nicky Butt running down the right-hand side.
Is it a goal?
I'm afraid Butt has knocked out Batman,
Ow! That's got to hurt.
And here's Ruud Van Nistleroy,
Goal!
Manchester United are one-nil up.
But here comes some subs,
The Flintstones,
Let's see what they can do.
And here's Roy Keane -
A fantastic goal.
Two-nil - the end of the match,
Manchester United top of the table.
Second - Tom and Jerry!

Ryan Johnson (8)
St Peter And St Paul Primary School, Bexhill-on-Sea

I Hope For Snow

I've got my sledge,
All bright and new,
On this cold and wintry day,
I hope and wish for snow to fall,
So I can go and play.
The sky is white,
The grass is white,
Yippee, it's time to go.

Matthew Fryer (8)
St Peter And St Paul Primary School, Bexhill-on-Sea

Go And Open The Door . . .

Go and open the door
Perhaps you'll see

Cars zooming past
Birds singing

Or maybe you'll see

A two headed, six legged, eight armed monster
All blood sucking and boneless
With no skin - no flesh
Eating everything like fools.

But don't be afraid
Go and open the door.

Daniel Gardner (7)
St Peter And St Paul Primary School, Bexhill-on-Sea

Go And Open The Door . . .

Go and open the door
Perhaps you'll see

A tall, silver and yellow lamp post shining
And a dog barking at it - how silly!

Or maybe you'll see

A ghost skipping along the path
A bony skeleton walking across the rooftops!

But don't be afraid
Go and open the door.

Paige Edwards (8)
St Peter And St Paul Primary School, Bexhill-on-Sea

Go And Open The Door . . .

Go and open the door
Perhaps you'll see

A little butterfly singing in a tree
Or a dog barking gleefully!

Or maybe you'll see

A bony skeleton walking to your house
A ghost skipping on the path, as quiet as a mouse
And now let's see
There's a bee, with a broken knee.

But don't be afraid
Go and open the door
See what you can see.

Chloe Willis (7)
St Peter And St Paul Primary School, Bexhill-on-Sea

Go And Open The Door . . .

Go and open the door
Perhaps you'll see

A boy running along the pavement
A car driving down the road

Or maybe you'll see

A vicious monster waiting to eat you up
A giant with huge feet, standing in the road

But don't be afraid
Go and open the door.

Connor Coshall (7)
St Peter And St Paul Primary School, Bexhill-on-Sea

Go And Open The Door . . .

Go and open the door
Perhaps you'll see

A brown and white dog
Barking at a person running

Or maybe you'll see

An alien running down the road
A flying saucer

But don't be afraid
Go and open the door.

Go and open the door
Perhaps you'll hear

A person singing
And a dog barking

Or maybe you'll hear

An alien singing
And a fat, hairy monster roaring

But don't be afraid
Go and open the door.

Go and open the door
Perhaps you will go

To the desert in India
To a school in Africa

Or maybe you'll go

To outer space
Swimming in the monster's slime

But don't be afraid
Go and see!

Thomas Elphick (7)
St Peter And St Paul Primary School, Bexhill-on-Sea

Go And Open The Door . . .

Go and open the door
Perhaps you'll see

A brown and white dog
Barking at a person running

Or maybe you'll see

An alien running down the road
A flying saucer

But don't be afraid
Go and open the door.

Go and open the door
Perhaps you'll hear

A cat purring
A bird singing

Or maybe you'll hear

A dragon blowing fire
A monster singing

But don't be afraid
Go and open the door.

Nathan Lopez (7)
St Peter And St Paul Primary School, Bexhill-on-Sea

Through That Door . . .

Through that door
Is a sandy desert
Where camels wander
And lizards scurry
Where the snake slides across the sand
And buried far beneath them
An ancient castle
Where skeletons with broken bones live on.

Natasha Coda (8)
St Peter And St Paul Primary School, Bexhill-on-Sea

Go And Open The Door . . .

Go and open the door
Perhaps you'll see

Cars driving along the road
And birds singing in the air

Or maybe you'll see

A vampire levitating over the ground
Or an alien doing a handstand

But don't be afraid
Go and open the door.

Go and open the door
Perhaps you'll hear

The wind on your face
And rain dripping down the windowpane

Or maybe you'll hear

A flying saucer swooping through the air
Or a TV stamping on the ground

But don't be afraid
Go and open the door.

Owen Mitchell (8)
St Peter And St Paul Primary School, Bexhill-on-Sea

Teachers

After school's out
Teacher's turn into aliens
With five tentacles
And ten eyes.
The monsters love sugar cubes
For tea they have roasted kids
With sugar cubes and blood of humans
In the staff room.

George Kent (8)
St Peter And St Paul Primary School, Bexhill-on-Sea

Go And Open The Door . . .

Go and open the door
Perhaps you'll see

A sun beaming in the sky
A dog sniffing a tree,

Or maybe you'll see

A ten-eyed monster
Eating the cars and drinking the sea

But don't be afraid
Go and open the door.

Go and open the door
Perhaps you'll hear

The wind whistling through the trees
The car horns, *beep beeping* angrily

Or maybe you'll hear
A spaceship whizzing through the air
An alien singing a song and spiking his hair!

But don't be afraid
Go and open the door.

Shannon Eason (8)
St Peter And St Paul Primary School, Bexhill-on-Sea

Dinosaur World

I went to dinosaur world,
The sky was all orange and red,
Stamp, stamp, stamp, roar!
The ground shudders and shakes,
May be you'll go there one day.
The dinosaurs are really, really big,
Sharp teeth and long claws,
If you go there be careful,
Or otherwise you will be eaten!

Adam Dawes (7)
St Peter And St Paul Primary School, Bexhill-on-Sea

The Rugby World Cup

Jonny Wilkinson takes the ball
He's running down the wing
He's going to score
When he's tackled.
France has the ball.
Tackled again.
England on the run and they're fouled.
England takes the penalty
And . . .
He's done it
The ball goes 100 metres up
Over the bar
The crowd go mad
But they have to take the scrum
In it goes and out.
England has the ball again
But it's off - over the touchline.
France takes the throw in
It's done very quickly
But intercepted by Wilkinson
And kicked over the post
To score an outstanding *goal*
The fans go wild
England has won the World Cup!

James Hirst (8)
St Peter And St Paul Primary School, Bexhill-on-Sea

Through That Door

Through that door
Is a land of sweets,
Where jelly babies cry
And chocolate bars sing,
Where lolly lamps light up the roads,
For Malteser wheels to go round and round
And fruit winder snakes to slither through the grass.

Lalaine Nathan (7)
St Peter And St Paul Primary School, Bexhill-on-Sea

Go And Open The Door

Go and open the door
Perhaps you'll see
Apples hanging on a tree
A green jeep in the driveway
Or maybe you'll see
An alien in the tree house
A six-eyed monster eating ice cream
But don't be afraid
Go and open the door.

Henry Message (7)
St Peter And St Paul Primary School, Bexhill-on-Sea

Go And Open The Door

Go and open the door
Perhaps you'll see
A baby climbing the stairs
A man watching TV
Or maybe you'll see
A six-legged monster sipping Coca-Cola
A pink leopard driving a jeep
But don't be afraid
Go and open the door.

Keir Claridge (8)
St Peter And St Paul Primary School, Bexhill-on-Sea

Through That Door

Through that door is an underwater world
Where mermaids sing and swim,
And fish glide and dance through the waves.
Where dolphins go to school,
In beautiful blue wagons,
Swimming everywhere,
In and out of houses made from shells.

Lucy Whittaker (8)
St Peter And St Paul Primary School, Bexhill-on-Sea

Go And Open The Door

Go and open the door
Perhaps you'll see
A bright blue sky
Or the sun and the moon shining
Or maybe you'll see
A monster climbing up a tree
Or an alien spaceship landing on the ground
But don't be afraid
Go and open the door.

Christopher Ball (8)
St Peter And St Paul Primary School, Bexhill-on-Sea

Go And Open The Door

Go and open the door
Perhaps you'll see
A baby holding a flower
Trees blowing in the wind
Or maybe you'll see
A witch flying over the moon
Two little cats swimming in the pool
But don't be afraid
Go and open the door.

Teia Berwick (8)
St Peter And St Paul Primary School, Bexhill-on-Sea

Through That Door . . .

Through that door
Is the lonely mountain
Where a dragon lives
And treasure gleams
Where bones lie
And fire spouts.

Samuel Hirst (8)
St Peter And St Paul Primary School, Bexhill-on-Sea

Rain

Rain
Speeding rapidly
Faster and faster
Descending down the pane
Turning the whole universe gloomy
Suddenly a huge flash
An enormous roar
Like lions
Storm.

Jessica Adams (11)
St Peter And St Paul Primary School, Bexhill-on-Sea

Through That Door . . .

Through that door
Is a sandy desert
Where camels wander
And lizards scurry
Where the snake slides through the sand
And birds fly slowly in the air.

Jasmine Standley (8)
St Peter And St Paul Primary School, Bexhill-on-Sea

Wings Of Gold

Me
A bird
Wings of gold
Floating above the world
Watching time pass
A bird
Me.

Ella Wormley-Healing (10)
St Peter And St Paul Primary School, Bexhill-on-Sea

My Sparkling Winter

My winter shimmers and shines.
Snowmen and trees covered in white.
But the stars are the best,
Sparkling at their own height,
In the dark night,
While the winter magic flies through the night,
Covering the land in white!

Katie Richards (8)
St Peter And St Paul Primary School, Bexhill-on-Sea

The Orange

The orange,
Dark or light,
Ripe or unripe,
With a small green stalk like a little bush.
If you throw it, it looks like the sun,
Coming down like a meteor on fire,
Swirling and turning.
With marks like little countries on Earth,
And an orange sea
Sharp or sweet it still fills your tummy.

Christian Pestell (7)
St Peter And St Paul Primary School, Bexhill-on-Sea

The Things

Teddy bears are cuddly and cute,
Butterflies are brightly coloured,
Cats say miaow,
Tigers are sweet and playful,
Yes, these are the things we like most.

Hollie Kinch (9)
St Peter And St Paul Primary School, Bexhill-on-Sea

Basketball

B asketball,
A s fast as a bullet,
S uper quick thinking,
K eeping the ball always moving,
E very attempt is a step further,
T ime is pressuring on you,
B all is speeding up,
A ll the time is running out,
L oudly the crowd cheers your team on,
L ast second dunk by Michael Jordan.

Samuel Ball (10)
St Peter And St Paul Primary School, Bexhill-on-Sea

Spring

Spring is a lovely time of year,
With blossoms on every tree.

Grass is growing in different shades,
Roses are jumping out,
This is nature Wow! Wow! Wow!

Lambs are born sh, sh, sh!
Come on children let's go feed the little lambs.

Charlie Hole (9)
St Peter And St Paul Primary School, Bexhill-on-Sea

Hot Cocoa

I cuddle up in the blanket next to the fire
When I'm at school people think I'm a liar
But when I am cuddled up by the fire with hot cocoa
I'm forgetting them already.

Hayley Bates (11)
St Peter And St Paul Primary School, Bexhill-on-Sea

Snow

Snow falls to the ground
No sound but silence
Colder and colder every second
Ice and frost stick together
White, white everything white
All sparkling in the sun
Slippery children slipping around
It's the time that's lots of fun.

Gemma Hawkes (10)
St Peter And St Paul Primary School, Bexhill-on-Sea

The Chattering Seat

As I lay on my bed with the dog on my feet
I heard the sound of a chattering seat
Scared, I shivered
Shook and jibbered
The wind started howling
The dog started growling
All of a sudden I heard a cackling in my head
Oh no, it's just a dream, I am in my bed.

Kyle Coleman (11)
St Peter And St Paul Primary School, Bexhill-on-Sea

School Dinners

Everybody hates school dinners,
Mushy peas and soggy fish fingers,
Everybody hates school dinners,
Lumpy custard and dead bits of skin,
Everybody hates school dinners,
Hard chips and greasy burgers,
Everybody hates school dinners.

Amy Norman (11)
St Peter And St Paul Primary School, Bexhill-on-Sea

My Horrible Week

On Monday 1st of May,
I had a really horrible day.
My friends were mean,
As mean as a teacher!

On Tuesday 2nd of May
I had another horrible day.
My teacher told me off for talking,
And made me stay in for my break.

On Wednesday 3rd of May,
I had yet another horrible day.
My dog died at only two,
And now I'm crying in my room.

On Thursday 4th of May,
I had another horrible day.
I was bullied by the elders,
And now I have a black eye.

On Friday 5th of May,
I had yet another horrible day.
My best friend left the school,
And now I'm on my own.

I've had a really horrible week!

Monday my friends were mean,
Tuesday the teacher told me off,
Wednesday my dog died,
Thursday I was bullied,
Friday my friend left the school.
I've had a horrible week!

Kellie Danielle Sallows (10)
St Peter And St Paul Primary School, Bexhill-on-Sea

My Piper's Deal!

A thousand guilders the mayor cried going pink
How about 50 and have a drink?
The piper sat down and talked
The corporation jumped up and hawked
The corporation and I will give you a deal
How about a 10 course meal?
The piper shook his head
And said just give me the thousand then I'll fled.

Jack Woodward (11)
St Peter And St Paul Primary School, Bexhill-on-Sea

Spring

Spring is coming,
Jump for joy,
Blossoms and roses,
Are bright and light,
Come on nature,
Grow, grow, grow,
Grass is growing,
In different shades.

Emma Blackford (8)
St Peter And St Paul Primary School, Bexhill-on-Sea

On The First Day Of School

I remember that day
We made pictures out of hay
We drew on the blackboard
We got all mucky
Mums were mad
They made us sad
We cried and cried until our hearts were content.

Sammy Langan (11)
St Peter And St Paul Primary School, Bexhill-on-Sea

Rocket

Get inside a rocket
Whoosh
We're off
Past the moon
There's Mars
Jupiter
Saturn
Uranus
Neptune
The jets are dying down
We're landing
Hooray!
We're on Pluto!

Ross Jackson (8)
St Peter And St Paul Primary School, Bexhill-on-Sea

The Monster

There was a monster in the school,
He was big,
He was hairy,
He was very scary.
He chased all the children,
He chased all the staff,
And went to the head's room where he had a bath.
After the bath he wanted his lunch,
The secretary looked tasty, quite a good munch.
He chewed and chewed but spat out the bone,
His work was done now, time to go home.

Connor Dunn (7)
St Peter And St Paul Primary School, Bexhill-on-Sea

The Mad Gardener's Song

He thought he saw a walking chair
Running out the door,
He looked again and found it was
Something on the floor,
'I think I'll go downstairs,' he said
'To have a little snore!'

He thought he saw an elephant
Chasing a big mouse,
He looked again and found it was
A tiny little louse,
'I think I'll scratch my head,' he said
'And go into my house!'

Oscar McAleese (9)
The Fold School

The Mad Gardener's Song

He thought he saw a giant dog,
Sitting on the house.
He looked again and found it was
A tiny little mouse.
'Would you go away,' he said,
'I'd rather have a grouse.'

He thought he saw an albatross,
Flying in the sun.
He looked again and found it was
The shadow of a bun.
'I think I'm going mad,' he said,
'I must go for a run.'

Harry Dale (8)
The Fold School

The Mad Gardener's Song

He thought he saw a red pigeon
On his way to school.
He looked again and found it was
A bouncing little ball.
'I think I'll go downstairs,' he said
'And make a little call!'

He thought he saw a blue piglet
Dancing in the hall.
He looked again and found it was
An ogre in mid fall.
'I think I'll go outside,' he said
'And play a little ball!'

He thought he saw a bouncing frog
Playing with a ball.
He looked again and found it was
A lizard on the wall.
'I think I'll go downstairs,' he said
'And play a little pool.'

Tom Gibson (8)
The Fold School

The Mad Gardener's Song

He thought he saw a grizzly bear
Dancing to cha cha,
He looked again and found it was
A knight in a black bar,
'I think I'm going mad,' he said,
'And then he said, 'ha, ha!'

He thought he saw a jewellery thief
That came from Hounslow Heath,
He looked again and found it was
His great-related niece,
'Would you like some cake?' he said,
'And have a little piece!'

Navraj Manku (9)
The Fold School

Young Writers - Once Upon A Rhyme East Sussex

The Mad Gardener's Song

He thought he saw a big old mule
Disobeying the law,
He looked again and found it was
A mouldy apple core,
'I think I'll go downstairs,' he said
'And try and have some more!'

He thought he saw a stripy ball
Dancing with the wall,
He looked again and found it was
An elephant being cool,
'I'll just go and see my friend,' he said
'And change my name to Paul!'

He thought he saw an elephant
Dancing with a pig,
He looked again and found it was
A hippo with a wig,
'I think I'm very mad,' he said
'I think I'm going to dig!'

Sammy Coleman (8)
The Fold School

The Mad Gardener's Song

He thought he saw a boxing frog
Kicking on the wall,
He looked again and found it was
A bouncing, springy ball,
'There's nothing in my head,' he said
'I'll play a little pool!'

Bradley Austin (8)
The Fold School

The Mad Gardener's Song

He thought he saw an aeroplane
Dancing on the floor,
He looked again and found it was
An ant upon the door,
'I think I'll leave him there,' he said
'Trying for the war!'

He thought he saw an old green brick
Playing on the wall,
He looked again and found it was
An old man being cool,
'I think I'm pretty mad,' he said
'I'll go into the pool!'

He thought he saw a jumping bin
Jumping round the street,
He looked again and found it was
An insect on the seat,
'I think he's very small,' he said
'I want something to eat!'

Reece Dakin (9)
The Fold School

The Mad Gardener's Song

He thought he saw a hairy plant
Sitting on a tree,
He looked again and found it was
A mouldy number three.
'I think I'll go downstairs,' he said
'And have a cup of tea!'

He thought he saw a little frog
Dancing on the wall,
He looked again, and found it was
An old man having a call,
'I think I'm pretty mad,' he said
'I'll go and play some ball!'

Jassem Al-Shehab (9)
The Fold School

Silver Sky

Reflections shimmer in my eyes
Silver birds fly by

Shiny moon moves around
Silent night not a sound

Shimmering waters look so smooth
Ghostly clouds slowly move

Shiny windows reflect on the floor
The silver moon seeks for more

The glowing sky lights up earth
A splinter of moon breaks the turf

The glimmering stars twinkle and wink
Conjuring up thoughts, making me think

Shiny moon moves around
Silent night, not a sound.

Rebecca Eaton (11)
Willingdon Primary School

My Winter Poem

Cold and frosty everywhere,
I snuggle close to my teddy bear,
Everyone else, fast asleep,
I creep out of bed to take a peek.

The garden pond is covered in ice,
The large tree's shadow cuts out a slice.
The grass is wearing a crisp white coat,
Slowly, gently snowflakes float.

No swooping birds in the sky,
Creeping low and fluttering high,
Rooftops no longer brown,
It's snowing everywhere in the town.

Samara Lynn (9)
Willingdon Primary School

Bunny Was Born

She took the branches of a tree,
Springing in the wind
To make her hop.

She stole the darkness of night
And the shininess of marbles
To make her eyes.

Rabbit made time stand still
When she took the ticking of the clock
For her twitchy nose.

From the gentle dropping of daffodil leaves
And the softness of silk,
She made her ears.

For her large, thumping back foot,
She used the beating of a drum
And the rhythm of music.

For her coat she took the fluffiness
Of a soft, woolly jumper
And the pure whiteness of just fallen snow.

Finally, she sat on a cotton wool ball
And made her soft white bobtail
And so, bunny was born.

Kyra Dinnage (9)
Willingdon Primary School

My Best Friend

Your best friend is someone who is always there,
Someone to lean on, someone to care,
Someone if you're angry, sad or in trouble,
Someone to talk to and have a cuddle.
If you're upset, worried or scared,
It's a nice feeling to know that someone is there.

Ellie Robinson (11)
Willingdon Primary School

How Elephant Began

Elephant began
He took a bent knitting needle
He took the moon for his ivory
And made his tusks

For his trunk
He took the length of a drainpipe
He took the colour from a stone
He took the moving of a palm tree

For his feet
He took the size from a dustbin lid
He took the colour from granite
He took the heaviness of a computer

For his skin
He took the feel of an old leather jacket
He took the colour from rain-filled clouds
He took the shine from the stars

For his eyes
He took the size from a marble
He took the colour from the sun
And elephant was made.

Charlotte Yates (9)
Willingdon Primary School

Silly Billy

I have a dog called Billy and he acts quite silly,
He has two big, round eyes, which look like pies,
He has two pointy ears that point out like spears,
His wet and shiny nose where it's been nobody knows,
He has four big, paddy paws and when he's asleep he snores,
And even though he's rather silly,
I do love my dog called Billy.

William Leeding (9)
Willingdon Primary School

My Family Of Weather

My mum is a rainbow, all sunny and bright,
My dad is the wind, calm and helpful.
One cat is like frost, cool and wise,
The other is like snow, crisp and playful.
My sister is a cloud and drifts with happiness,
I am the sun, warm and comforting.

I have fun every day with my family they're here to stay,
Dancing and playing all the time,
What a different family I have.

My auntie is like rain, kind and refreshing,
My uncle is a white cloud, happy on every occasion.
My nan is a breeze, who gently touches us all,
My grandad is the moon, bright and colourful.
My cousin is a tornado and holds happy memories,
My other cousin is the wind who sways in a peaceful way.

I have fun every day with my family they're here to stay,
Dancing and playing all the time,
What a different family I have.

Rebecca Triggs (10)
Willingdon Primary School

Family Pets

Dogs have paws, a nose and tail
And like water but not hail

Cats like a warm, cosy bed
And a growling dog they really dread

Rabbits wriggle their little pink nose
Searching for a luscious rose

Chinchillas run about the place
And often are in disgrace

Gerbils like fingers and food
And are often in a very good mood.

Charlotte Golding (9)
Willingdon Primary School

11th Of November

On the 11th day of the 11th month we stop and remember
The people who died before the 11th of November,
Red poppies we wear, the colour of blood,
Tears flow down people's cheeks as if in a flood.

All the families broken and scattered around,
The dead, once loved bodies never to be found.
Mothers wait eagerly for happier news,
People watching TV desperately searching for clues.

Others all say why did it have to be him?
To lose a young father is such a horrible sin.
Families left without a son, brother or dad,
The sorrow they feel isn't just sad.

On the 11th day of the 11th month we stop and remember
The people who died before the 11th of November,
Red poppies we wear, the colour of blood,
Tears flow down people's cheeks as if in a flood.

Emma Le Teace (9)
Willingdon Primary School

Autumn Senses

Crinkling leaves go crunch under your feet,
Cold, grey days are not a treat.
Sparkling fireworks in the air,
Green, brown, red leaves everywhere.

Smell of bonfires fill the sky,
The hot taste of apple pie.
Hats, scarves, gloves to keep out the cold,
Plough the wheat before it's too old.
Use our senses to find out
What our world's all about.

Emily Ritchie (10)
Willingdon Primary School